The publication of this book
was made possible in part,
through a generous contribution
from Joseph Beth Booksellers.

PLAYHOUSE SQUARE

CLEVELAND

AN ENTERTAINING
HISTORY

1810 TO THE 21ST CENTURY

"A GLORIOUS
DRAMATIC PAGEANT..."

1810

THE POPULATION OF CLEVELAND IS 57 PEOPLE.
Euclid Avenue is an Indian trail and buffalo path. A century later, the city
will be a thriving metropolis with a Euclid Avenue that is as famous as New
York's Fifth Avenue. The years between are almost a blur in the rapidity with
which the city grows. From wilderness to farmland to a city of quiet elegance
to a bustling center of commerce – Cleveland moves inexorably toward the
twentieth century. Along the way, the population works and builds, makes
money and looks for ways to spend it. Some of it is spent for entertainment,
and theater entrepreneurs are born early in Cleveland, which soon becomes
… *a city of "playhouses".*

1820

The first performance of a professional touring company is given at Mowry's
Tavern, near Public Square, and The Shakespeare Gallery at No.1 Superior
gives occasional stage performances. The population of the city is 606.

Below: Cleveland
in 1800.

Above: Northwest corner of Public Square, 1831.

1836

The first theater license is granted to the Dean and McKinney Theatre on Superior and Union Lane, and *Hamlet* is produced. By now, Cleveland is an incorporated city with a population of 9,000 people and is included on the circuit of traveling entertainers from the East (although appearances are infrequent). Theatrical performances are usually held on the upper floors of commercial buildings.

THE 1850s

Cleveland begins to grow substantially during this decade. Euclid Avenue is now a very pretty residential street unmarred by the presence of storefronts, but there is also a thriving commerical district on Superior Street west of Public Square. The city has three daily newspapers, including *The Plain Dealer* and two weeklies, all of them formulated along political lines. This is a period of great dissent in America, manifested by the strife between North and South. Ohio is a center for tremendous political activity with strong suffragette and abolitionist organizations. There are many Cleveland citizens who provide havens for the fugitive slaves traveling the "Underground Railroad".

Nevertheless, even during this era of tremendous ferment, culture reaches new heights in the city, **especially with the founding of Cleveland University in 1850** and the opening of a beautiful playhouse in 1853.

1853

The Cleveland Theatre opens on the third floor of the building at 1371 W. 6th Street. John Ellsler, who will become one of Cleveland's major theatrical entrepreneurs, leases the Cleveland, renaming it the Academy of Music. He establishes a stock company which becomes one of the first drama schools in the country. The theater's ticket prices range from 25 cents in the balcony to an outrageous $10 for a box seat. Here at the Academy **John Wilkes Booth would play his last role prior to his infamous performance in Ford's Theatre in Washington, when he assassinates President Lincoln.** Performers at the Academy of Music also include James O'Neill (Eugene's father) in the role of Edmond Dantes in Monte Christo.

Above: Academy of Music. Right: John Wilkes Booth. Below: Lyceum Theatre (former Park Theatre) and Old Stone Church, c. 1889.

THE 1860s

The population of Cleveland has increased to 43,417 by 1860, more than a 250% increase over 1850. Some 44% of the city's populace is of foreign origins, as an ever-increasing number of immigrants become attracted to Cleveland's prosperity.

Then in 1861 the country is plunged into civil war; and like most of the nation, Cleveland is affected by the scarcity of hard money and plummeting wages. Education, cultural activities and sports are interrupted. At the end of the war, Cleveland has not only its dead soldiers but its assassinated President, Abraham Lincoln, to mourn. It is with relief that the city moves with the rest of the nation toward the work of reconstruction. Symbolically, a huge bell raised in the tower of the Old Stone Church is inscribed with the words: *Cast for the First Presbyterian Church, Cleveland, Ohio / In the Year of Peace, 1865.*

TRIVIA

In 1876, American artist **Archibald Willard**, best known for his patriotic paintings, moved to Cleveland and set up a studio overlooking Euclid Avenue where he painted his famous, "Spirit of '76."

THE 1870s

The decade following the Civil War is characterized by a nationwide sentimentality which reaches an apex in 1876 with the celebration of the 100th anniversary of the nation's founding. The country is also feeling the effects of "progress" since the 1869 joining of the tracks of the Central Pacific and Union Pacific lines. The opposite shores of the United States are now a short seven-day journey apart! Suddenly there is an acceleration of commerce all over the country, and like many cities, Cleveland feels the effects of new wealth.

The 1870s usher in a "golden age" for Euclid Avenue. The street has become a stretch of grand mansions with grounds sometimes extending as far as Lake Erie and elm trees arching over the avenue. This is "Millionaire's Row," where all the best families live; and among the more fashionable pursuits on Euclid Avenue are sleigh races in the winter and bicycling in the summer. But even the wealthy indulge occasionally in wicked entertainments like the popular "varieties," which are hodgepodges of songs, dance, comedy skits and specialty acts. The most famous house in Cleveland for the "varieties" is the Theatre Comique, and it is reputed that "no

Above: Elm trees lining Euclid Avenue, 1870. Below left: The Samuel Mather house; Euclid Avenue and 13th Street. Below right: The Tyler mansion; later to become site of the Bulkley Building.

Above left: The Euclid
Avenue Opera House
Playbill. Above right: The
Euclid Avenue Opera
House. Opposite page:
Park Theatre Programme,
1883.

more wicked place of amusement ever existed in
Cleveland." (Later the varieties will be cleaned up for family consumption and called vaudeville or spiced with blue
humor and labeled burlesque.)

During the 70s and 80s theater also becomes big-
league entertainment, and performers like John Drew
and William Gillette achieve "star" billing. The city of
Cleveland builds a number of theaters during this period,
and they all feature the light comedies and melodramatic
extravaganzas which the ticket-buying masses prefer.

1875

John Ellsler opens the Euclid Avenue Opera House at
E.4th and Euclid and moves his stock company from the
Academy of Music. The Opera House, considered to be
one of the finest playhouses in the country, has an interi-

or ornamented with crimson velvet, fine paintings, luxurious carpets and a massive chandelier. Opening night is an exciting theatrical event for Cleveland, and society flocks to the theater for a performance of *Saratoga*. In 1879, Ellsler is forced to sell the theater, but it is bought by Marcus A. Hanna, who retains its elegance and distinction. (The Opera House is destroyed by fire in 1892 but Hanna rebuilds it.) For many years, the Euclid Avenue Opera House remains Cleveland's most prestigious legitimate theater, featuring performances by such actors as Edwin Booth and Anna Held, operas presented by the Metropolitan, and later, the Ziegfield Follies.

1883

John Ellsler next opens the Park Theatre as part of the three-story Wick Block erected on Public Square (later the site of the Illuminating Co.) The opening features the comedy, *School for Scandal*, and the event is marked with "splendor and social importance." The Park continues to present the best theater groups and opera companies.

PARK THEATRE PROGRAMME.

Programme for this Monday Eve'g.
Oct. 22   1883

M'LLE RHEA,

SUPPORTED BY

Mr. Wm. Harris,

And a Carefully Selected Company under the Management of

MR. ARTHUR B. CHASE,

Will present M'lle Rhea's own version of the Delightful Play, Entitled

THE SCHOOL FOR SCANDAL.

Cast of Characters:

LADY TEAZLE, ... M'LLE RHEA
Charles Surface, ... Mr. Wm. Harris
Sir Peter Teazle .... Robert G. Wilson
Sir Oliver .... George Woodward
Careless .... W. G. Reynier
Joseph Surface .... John T. Sullivan
Crabtree, }
Moses,   }
Sir Benjamin Backbite, ... Leo Cooper
Rowley .... J. R. Amory
Snake .... Owen Ferree
Trip .... C. N. Drew
Mrs. Candour .... Edwin Davies
Lady Sneerwell .... Mrs. Ella Wren
Maria .... Miss Eugenie Lindeman
Owen Ferree .... Gracie Hall
.... Stage Manager for M'lle Rhea

EXCERPT FROM AN ARTICLE ENTITLED:

"History of the Stage from 1820-1893"

IN THE CLEVELAND AMUSEMENT GAZETTE OF DECEMBER 16, 1893:

There are many younger People who still remember the dirty old hell-hole of iniquity Frankfort Street, just back of the Weddell House, that was known in the last years of its existence as the Theatre Comique...

It was a place where men could go back of stage and form the acquaintance of the actresses; and in course of time it was an eye-sore and one of the plague spots of the city. Wickedness in its worst form is the nightly program back of its dingy walls, and the admission price being small, many a boy took his first lesson in vice in that pest-house called a theatre ... Beer and other drinks were sold while the performances were in progress. Young boys were seen smoking cigars and vile pipes, and occasionally the city council made a spasmodic effort to change matters, but it was to no avail, for in a short time the old place would return to the can-can and other indecencies that flourished in those days. . . .

What good news that was to the mothers and fathers of Cleveland when that wicked old place was finally leveled to the ground.

— M. WEIDENTHAL

1885

Charles H. Bulkley builds the Cleveland Theatre on the corner of Ontario and St. Clair which opens on October 19th, 1885 with Michael Strogoff in *Courier of the Czar,* "a glorious dramatic and military pageant in five acts and ten tableaux, interspersed with grand ballet divertissement with 150 persons on stage."

In 1886 the "Cleveland" is taken over by H. R. Jacobs, who opens his first season with *Lights 0' London.* The H. R. Jacobs Cleveland Theatre features a mixture of melodrama, comedy and comic opera. In 1892, when the theater is re-opened after having been badly damaged by fire, it is called the H. R. Jacobs Theatre. But the name is short-lived, when in 1894 it changes hands and again becomes the Cleveland Theatre. Enter an era of gory melodrama which lasts until March 6, 1910 with the playing of *The Elsie Siegel Chinese Trunk Mystery Case.* Cheap vaudeville and moving pictures become the staple of the theater until its closing.

Above: The H. R. Jacobs Theatre. Below: The Star Theatre. Right: The H.R. Jacobs Theatre Program Masthead.

1887

The Columbia Theatre opens at E. 4th and Euclid on September 12th, 1887. Playgoers climb into shays and drive from the farther reaches of the city to attend the premiere of Hanlon's Fantasma. The Columbia is primarily a vaudeville house which features the favorite stars of the day, including James A. Heine and Maude Banks.

1889

The Columbia becomes The Star, with vaudeville, melo-

drama and comic opera predominating until the 1890s, when burlesque is introduced. Big names like Weber and Fields play here. The Park Theatre on Public Square becomes the Lyceum on September 2nd. A variety of attractions of a popular character are presented at somewhat lower prices than the Euclid Avenue Opera House, but **the Lyceum still manages to bring to Cleveland great performers like Sara Bernhardt, Lillian Russell and Luisa Lane Drew (grandmother of Lionel, Ethel and John Barrymore and great-great grandmother of Drew Barrymore).**

THE 1890s

The gay 90s are a decade of growth for Cleveland, which celebrates its 100th birthday in 1896. Cleveland is now the 10th largest city in the nation, with an increase of 600% over the population figure of 1860, and the changing character of Euclid Avenue reflects the city's tremendous growth. The towering elm trees along Euclid begin to disappear as the dirt road is paved with sandstone. Mansions are being bought by businessmen and torn down to make way for commercial ventures.

Streetcar lines on the once totally residential street hasten the transformation to a business avenue. Already the commercial district has progressed toward Ninth Street and wealthy families are moving farther out Euclid Avenue.

For the upper and middle classes, this is the era of the Gibson Girl, sedate socials with cards and magic lantern shows for entertainment, buggy riding, and patronage of the arts. In Cleveland, an organization called the Old Bohemians fosters art appreciation, and in 1895 forty of the city's musicians found an early Cleveland Orchestra (not to be confused with the later group). Audiences gather for concerts on Sunday afternoons in Gray's Armory, built in 1893 to house public events. Theater audiences are also out in full force – but not always sedately!

Above: The Lyceum Theatre. Left: Lillian Russell. Below: Arch erected 1896 in Public Square on Superior Avenue to celebrate Cleveland's centennial.

Above left: The Euclid Avenue
Presbyterian Church stands on
the site of present day Hanna
Building. Above right: Parade
at Euclid Avenue and E. 9th.
Below right: Grays Armory.
Left: Actress and "Gibson Girl"
Nanette Comstock.

During the 1890s the shows in Cleveland get bigger
and gaudier, and so do the crowds! Vaudeville, circuses
and gory melodramas are popular. Burlesque is introduced, and "flickers" are shown in storeroom theaters for
5 cent admission. These early movies are projections on a
white sheet shown to the accompaniment of piano music.
The marvelous new invention of these "moving pictures"
during the latter part of the nineteenth century heralds
the beginning of a century of inventions.

TWENTIETH
CENTURY

1900

Pre-Playhouse Square area, from East 14th to East 17th St. Hotel Fuller sits on site of present day Palace Theatre, 1914.

AT THE TURN OF THE CENTURY only 18 people in every 1,000 own the new-fangled telephone. There is no such thing as a radio or an electric icebox. In many ways, America is still rural, with 11 million of its people working as farmers. Yet at the same time, over 6 million are already employed in factories, and countless new inventions will soon affect the very nature of the American way of life. The attitude of much of the country toward the new changes is summed up by Senator Mark Hanna of Ohio: "Furnaces are glowing, spindles are singing their song. Happiness comes to us all with prosperity."

The Union Club, Cleveland, Ohio.

Above: The Union
Club. Bottom left:
The Statler Hotel,
1905.

Euclid Avenue is rapidly becoming a boulevard of elegant hotels, restaurants and fashionable shops. Mansions from 9th to 18th streets are torn down, and the eastward progression of the commercial district continues. The Statler Hotel and the Union Club are built at 12th and Euclid around 1905 and the Sterling Welch home furnishings store in 1909. Then in 1910 four beautiful homes in the 13th Street block are leveled and a huge department store called Higbee's is built at the corner of 13th. Halle Bros. builds across the street. **(The Halle architect is Henry Bacon, who later will design the Lincoln Memorial in Washington, D.C.)**

Meanwhile, beginning in 1900, several new theaters are built on Euclid, Superior, Prospect and Huron, creating a strong concentration of entertainment facilities in downtown. These theaters will feature everything from legitimate stage productions (at an all-time high across the country), and vaudeville (still the favorite entertainment). The "flicks" are still shown in storefront nickelodeons.

Above left: The Halle Building, c. 1910. Above right: The center court of the Sterling & Welch Co, c. 1909. Bottom: Intersection of Euclid Ave. and Huron Rd.

The Empire Theatre opens on Huron Road (on the later site of the Ohio Bell Building) and features "high-class, fashionable vaudeville." Managed by Max Faetkenheuer, a well-known theater name in Cleveland, the Empire presents so many stars that the shows are called "the headliners of America." The theater also features Shakespearean and classical presentations starring William Farnurn and his stock company. He proves so popular that ticket holders line up all the way to Erie (Ninth Street).

1903

The Colonial Theatre opens on Superior just west of E. 6th Street on March 16th. Max Faetkenheuer directs the orchestra and Nora Bayes is the vaudeville headliner. The Colonial features several successful seasons of "The Vaughan Glaser Stock Company", until, in 1918, the theater becomes the Shubert-Colonial and Shubert road shows are booked.

1904

The Prospect Theatre opens just east of the Colonial Arcade on Prospect. It becomes the first B.F. Keith vaudeville house in Cleveland when Keith buys it in 1905. Later, when he takes over the "Hipp", the Prospect becomes a cheap vaudeville house. The Wonderland Theatre, on the ground floor of the Ellington Apts. on the west side of E. 9th St. at Superior Ave. N.E., is one of several nickelodeons run by Max Lefkowich during the early 1900s.

Above left: The Empire
Theatre. Middle left:
The Colonial Theatre.
Bottom left: The
Prospect Theatre.

1908

The Hippodrome Building, including the huge Hippodrome Theatre, opens. It is a unique structure with an eleven-story section facing Euclid Avenue and a seven-story section facing Prospect. The Hippodrome Theatre stretches between the two avenues, and people come from long distances to see this immense playhouse, which now ranks among the world's greatest. The opening production in the Hippodrome is the musical *Coaching Days,* and the feature of the evening is the exciting spectacle of horses diving into a large water tank built into the front of the stage. Presentations at the Hipp now and after Keith takes over the theater include grand opera, popular musical shows, vaudeville and movies. **John Phillip Sousa and Marie Dressler are two of the many name performers who play the "Hipp".**

Above: The Wonderland Theatre.
Below: The Hippodrome
Building. Bottom left: B.F.
Keith's Hippodrome Program.

Above: Actress Anna Held,
Florence Ziegfield's first wife
and the popular Ziefgield
Follies gal who became famous
for her milk baths. Below:
Playbill for Miss Hanna Held.

THE 1910s

This will not be the decade to bear out the optimism expressed by Senator Hanna during the first decade of the new century. In some respects, it is one of the ugliest periods in American history, characterized by race riots and mob lynchings of radicals. The plight of the common laborer reaches an all-time high, and workers begin to rebel against subsistence wages. Meanwhile, the first World War casts a shadow across the nation.

Paradoxically, the entertainment industry thrives and, in fact, its glamour reflects the inequities of the period. New York's "Broadway" is now the entertainment capital of America, with some three dozen marquees ablaze each night. There are a few dramas, but the public generally prefers comedy, music and spectacle. The incredibly lavish Ziegfield Follies characterize the American taste of the period.

While Broadway shows on tour are drawing droves of people in cities across the country, movies are also becoming fashionable now. Some 25 million people a day attend movies featuring their favorite stars, some of whom are paid enormous weekly salaries. The silent films of the era are mostly melodramatic serials, extravaganzas a la Cecil B. De Mille, madcap comedies like the Keystone Kops and syrupy romances which feature leading movie queens like Mary Pickford.

In keeping with the increasingly extravagant entertainment, the theaters being built during this decade are lavish showcases of gilded columns, plush seats, uniformed ushers and huge orchestras. People flock to these "palaces" in awe and delight.

In Cleveland several lavish theaters are planned for vaudeville and movies, but cultural groups also flourish on a smaller scale. In 1915 the Playhouse Settlement is founded by Russell and Rowena Jelliffe "for the purpose of overcoming racial conflict through the medium of the cultural arts." **A theater group called the Gilpin Players is formed, housed on E. 38th and Central and called Karamu Theatre.** Uptown, in a church at E. 73rd and Cedar, a group called the Play House Company is organized in

1916 "for the purpose of establishing an art theater." (In
**1926 The Cleveland Play House, now one of the major
regional theatres in the country, will receive a new home
on E. 86th Street.) And in 1918 the Cleveland Orchestra
is formed by the Musical Arts Association and presents its
first concert in Gray's Armory. (Our world-renowned
symphony orchestra is given a permanent home in 1931
in the University Circle area.)** Meanwhile downtown,
entertainment entrepreneurs move into full gear.

1914

Joseph Laronge, who becomes known as one of the
greatest real estate developers of his time, builds the Mall
Theatre near Public Square and the Euclid Theatre at
9th and Euclid. The Mall takes advantage of the two
main traffic arteries of the city with an entrance on
Euclid and one off Superior. Both the Euclid and the
Mall run movies; the Euclid also features a full orchestra
on a moving stage (again led by Max Faetkenheuer!).

Above: The Cleveland Orchestra
at Gray's Armory, November 13,
1919. Below: Cleveland
Symphony Orchestra Playbill.

Above: Joseph Laronge.
Below: Electric light
display on East 13th St.
Bottom: Bulkley Building
and Allen Theatre during
construction, 1920.

Neither theater becomes a first-run house, however, since neither is owned by a national syndicate.

Also during 1914 the Cleveland Electrical Exposition is held at Wigmore's Coliseum on 13th Street right off Euclid Avenue. **Thomas Edison presses the button that starts the machinery for the impressive displays that win Cleveland national acclaim as the "first city" in the electrical industry.**

1916

The first theater is built in the area that will become Playhouse Square. It is the Stillman at E. 12th and Euclid, and is one of the most elaborate motion-picture houses in the nation. The seating capacity is 1,800, and it books the leading pictures of the times.

By now this area is ripe for development. For Laronge, the Stillman is just the beginning. He envisions the Euclid Avenue district from 9th to 17th as an elegant promenade, including restaurants, fine shops and a line of magnificent playhouses. So in 1916, Laronge presents his plans for the area to leaders in the theatrical business and suggests strategic locations. Laronge, two men named Strong and Desberg and Marcus Loew form a partnership called "Loew's Ohio Theatres," with the result that in five years several beautiful playhouses are completed or under construction, and a unique "city-planning" concept results in the entertainment district known as ... **PLAYHOUSE SQUARE.**

PLAYHOUSE SQUARE

1920

CHRISTENED THE "JAZZ AGE," this decade is dominated by a spirit of frivolity. A spectacular economic boom has created a more materialistic attitude in American society, and the 1920 Prohibition Amendment inspires a kind of unrestrained hedonism among the rich. Entertainment is at an all-time high, with the emphasis on the glamorous, the extravagant. Movies are more sophisticated, costumes more exotic, and sex much more obvious. Vaudeville is still popular, with the lush Ziegfeld Follies as the ultimate representation of this entertainment. Jazz orchestras are the rage in the speakeasies and the big theaters. And as for legitimate theater, the plays are overwhelmingly "escapist".

Below: Playhouse Square during construction of Allen Theatre, 1921, one year prior to construction of Palace Theatre and Keith Building.

Above: Grand Lobby of State Theatre, 1921. Below: State Theatre Auditorium, 1921. Inset: Glass lantern slide of State Theatre's opening feature film.

In Cleveland, the Indians win the World Series in 1920; Public Auditorium opens in 1922 for conventions, expositions and entertainments; the rum runners are active on Lake Erie; and everyone comes downtown for their good times, especially after a building boom in Playhouse Square creates the most exciting entertainment area the city has yet seen!

1920s
THE BOOM BEGINS!

During 1920, construction begins on two new theaters in Playhouse Square. The State and the Ohio (in the 15th Street block) have only an 85-foot frontage on Euclid Avenue, but the property on which the theaters are located has a 500-foot depth. Both theaters, particularly the State, are characterized by their long, beautifully appointed lobbies. **The two open within a week of each other, the State premiering on February 5th, 1921 with a movie and the Ohio making its debut on February 14, 1921 as a legitimate theater.**

The State Theatre, which opens under the auspices of the "Loew's Ohio Theatres" partnership, is actually located on E. 17th Street, but the building of one of the longest lobbies in the world gives the theatrer the desired Euclid Avenue frontage. The State's opening is a gala affair, with Marcus Loew bringing in two special trainloads of film celebrities to attend the festivities.

Opening night guests enjoy the movie *Polly with a Past* and the Buster Keaton short *Neighbors*. In the pit is the Hyman L. Spitalny Orchestra. This combination of movies and orchestras becomes the formula for the State for several years.

EXCERPTS FROM AN ARTICLE IN THE WASHINGTON POST, FEB. 9, 1972:

"Though purists may still hold their noses, the Golden Age of the movie palace was a highpoint of American architecture. It is the daring, I think, that engendered the love, the daring of the old movie palaces to realize the splendor and dizzy luxury they crossed the ocean for. And it is that daring that makes these gaudy temples a highpoint of American architecture. The 300 or so truly great movie palaces across the continent were built in the short span between the coming of Prohibition and the onset of the Depression. They were built to please, nay to exult, a massive public taste, a popular yearning for illusion and fantasy and gaudy munificence. And in that sense, one might say, they were far more than "cathedrals of the motion picture. "They were temples of the people. And the people loved them.

The great movie palace architects did not, of course, create a new architecture. But with a weird inventiveness, they created new, fantastic illusions, concocted of, stolen from every conceivable architectural style of the past. Nothing was sacred. They stole architectural and ornamental motives with equal abandon from Romanesque Cathedrals and Angkor Wat, from Scheherazade's boudoir and Marie Antoinette's salon.

But it took creative daring to compose these architectural symphonies of minarets, gazebos, trellises, arches, cherubim and seraphim, more often than not made of genuine and costly material -bronze and marble and real Persian tiles – and stuffed with creditable works of art, furniture, rugs and fixtures.

Only a few of the old palaces have survived, though they were solidly built, often with exquisite craftsmanship... But the speculative builders and urban renewers are rapidly spelling the end of even the memory of a preposterous, gaudy, phony and beautiful Part of America's greatness."

—WOLF VON ECKARDT

JAMES DAUGHERTY

THE MAGNIFICENT MURALS WHICH cover the walls of the State Theatre lobby were painted during the early twenties by James Daugherty, an important American modernist whose works hang in the Museum of Modern Art, the Whitney and the Smithsonian.

Born in Asheville, North Carolina, Daugherty began studying art at the Corcoran Art School in Washington in 1906. He later studied at the Philadelphia Art Academy and abroad. About 1915 Daugherty became absorbed in color abstraction. According to the *N.Y. Times,* he was "an early nonobjective artist of the synchromist school, which structured paintings by means of flat planes and disks of brilliant color."

After 1920, Daugherty turned to mural paint-ing, portraying, especially, exciting themes from American history. The murals in the State lobby are, perhaps, the most striking examples of his work in this area. During the Thirties the artist began to illustrate children's books, doing the artwork for over fifty books and writing a dozen of his own. Many of his tales were inspired by farm stories he heard from his grandfather. In 1940, his book, "Daniel Boone" won the John Newberry medal for the year's most distinguished contribution to American literature for children.

In 1973, when the Playhouse Square Cabaret opened in the State lobby, the Association wrote a letter to Daugherty, telling him of the attempt to save the theaters, including the murals on which he had worked for three continuous months while the State was being finished. He wrote back a delightful letter, expressing his joy that the murals would be seen by the public again. "The whole project is so imaginative – a stunning achievement," he said. "To have my murals enhance again so gay and lively a scene after their long entombment is like something out of the Arabian nights – and evidently so practical a success! The whole thing a creation of inspiration and genius! Perhaps you have started a Cleveland renaissance a new cultural era of the Middle West…

James Daugherty died on February 21st, 1974, at the age of 84. For Clevelanders, his vibrant murals remain a most valuable aspect of a potential renaissance he would delight to see.

Above: "The Spirit of Fantasy –
Asia," mural in State Theatre grand
lobby (photo taken in 1973).
Center left: The State Theatre's
"Spirit of Cinema – America" mural
was featured on the cover of *Life*
Magazine on February 20, 1970.
Below left: Details from "The Spirit
of Drama – Europe." Below right:
James Daugherty in State Lobby
painting "The Spirit of Fantasy –
Asia," in 1921.

Faithful to her Destiny

Cleveland grows in greatness of strength and wealth and beauty. This superb playhouse, dedicated to art and happiness – is eloquent of her progress. Step by step we move forward, gaining each day firmer faith in the city that is yours and mine.

I delight in this new theatre, in the splendid development of Euclid avenue, in the numerous evidences that Cleveland has vision and the power to make her vision come true. I am pleased that I have had a part in these developments – the more so because all that my associates and I have accomplished is but a start. Changing just one of John Paul Jones' words – "We have only begun to go."

Joseph Laronge

Above left: "Faithful to her Destiny" by Joseph Laronge. Above right: Ohio Theatre marquee, c. 1920's. Below: The Ohio Theatre Opening Night Playbill, 1921

The Ohio next door is a 1338-seat house for the legitimate stage. Laronge and his partners open it in 1921 without Marcus Loew, but the Loew's chain takes over its management in 1922. The Ohio opens with a play called *The Return of Peter Grimm*, starring David Warfield. Generally, the Ohio books out-of-town dramatic and musical shows, everything from Eugene O'Neill's *Strange Interlude* to the Ziegfeld Follies. During the summer, "a repertory company of distinction" is featured.

TRIVIA

In 1920 as the Loew's chain anticipated building at Playhouse Square, they discovered there wasn't sufficient room to build two theaters in the space available. Since it was important that the marquees for their proposed venues have their marquees located on Euclid Avenue, an architectural plan was devised. The State was to be constructed *behind* the Palace (thereby necessitating the State's 320-ft. long lobby), while the Ohio would be built alongside the State, giving both theaters the desired Euclid Avenue frontage within a space of just 85 feet.

Above: The Ohio Theatre auditorium, 1921. Below: Grand Lobby of the Ohio Theatre, 1921.

Above: The Hanna Building, at East 14th and Euclid Avenue. Below: Hanna Theatre playbill. Inset: Allen Theatre opening day ad in Cleveland *Plain Dealer*.

The Hanna Theatre opens March 28th, 1921 as a legitimate theater and a replacement for the Euclid Avenue Opera House (which closes in 1922). The theater is housed in the Hanna Buildings, which cover over an acre and create the southeast corner of Playhouse Square on the site of the old Euclid Avenue Presbyterian Church. The complex is built by Dan R. Hanna in memory of his father Mark Hanna. Leading Shubert productions are brought into the Hanna during its opening season, which premieres on March 28th with *The Prince and the Pauper*.

During 1921, the construction of the Bulkley Building is also completed, including the impressive Allen Theatre. April 1st, the newest Playhouse Square theater opens with a twin bill of silent pictures: *The Greatest Love* starring Vera Gordan, and a comedy entitled *The Hallroom Boys*. The Allen has been built by Jule and Jay Allen, but in 1922 the Allen Brothers chain of theaters in Canada goes out of business and the Allen is taken over by the Loew's Corporation.

1921 clearly marks the year of "Playhouse Square", a title which is unofficially bestowed on the area by the newspapers. An organization called the Euclid Avenue Association, which has been founded to promote activities along the avenue from Public Square to University Circle, meets to ponder the issue of renaming Playhouse Square (a title they consider "frivolous"), and they hit upon the idea of calling it Euclid Square. But the unofficial title of "Playhouse Square" is the one that sticks.

Left: Allen Theatre Marquee, April 1921.

Below: Allen Theatre rotunda, 1921.

Bottom: Allen Theatre auditorium, stage with orchestra shell, 1921.

Above: Playhouse
Square Center, 1922.

1922

The highpoint of Playhouse Square development is the construction of the Keith Building and the two million dollar Palace Theatre, on the site of the old Dodge estate. **The largest electrical sign in the world advertises the theater atop the 21-story Keith Building.** Edward F. Albee builds the Palace as a monument to his vaudeville entrepreneur friend, B. F. Keith, and sets out to make the Palace "the showplace of the world". The beautiful "Grand Hall" of the Palace is appointed with treasures from all over the world and is hung with an enormously valuable art collection. Backstage offers every convenience to the performers in their dressing rooms, barber shop/beauty parlor, billiard room, nursery and lounges. The Palace is the swankiest vaudeville theater in the country, and all the big name performers "play the Palace". Its gala opening November 6, 1922 brings in New York society as well as Cleveland society, prominent officials of the

day, and celebrities galore. The headliner for the opening
bill is Elsie Janis, America's favorite mimic. She shares the
spotlight with the Cansinos, composed of Eduardo
(father of Rita Hayworth) Elisa, Angel and Jose, an aunt
and two uncles. Grace Hayes (mother of Peter Lind
Hayes) is also on the bill, along with a couple of hoofers,
some comedians, pantomimists and a big band.

Above: Keith Building, 1922.
Below: Palace Theatre Opening
Night ticket and souvenir
program, November 6, 1922.

B.F. KEITH'S PALACE THEATRE 1922
Opposite page (clockwise from top left): Palace Grand Hall stairway. Upper balcony "sky boxes." First floor Gentlemen's lounge (present day: Ladies Lounge). Palace Auditorium. Second Floor Ladies Lounge (present day: Boxholder's Lounge). This page top: Blue Sevres vase. Above left: Ladies Egyptian Smoking Room. Above right: Palace Main Floor Orchestra and Stage.

Above: Fanny Brice
during a live broadcast.
Below: Palace Theatre
newspaper ad.

The Twenties represent a pinnacle of entertainment activity in Cleveland. The Ohio, Hanna, Colonial (and the Play House farther uptown) all present legitimate stage productions. The downtown houses usually feature road shows of major New York hits, often starring the major performers of the day. There are some serious plays in each season's repertoire but, by and large, theater of the 20s is escapist fare. The ultimate example is the enormous hit *Abie's Irish Rose*, which opens at the Colonial September 10, 1923, a perfectly awful hearts and flowers romance which critics pan and audiences adore. The show runs in New York for five years and five months; and in Cleveland it has a 28-week run at the Colonial (a record which makes it the city's longest running show until October 31, 1973, when a production entitled *Jacques Brel is Alive and Well and Living in Paris* outdistances *Abie's Irish Rose*!)

The Ohio is presenting Ed Wynn in *The Perfect Foot* and the Hanna has the Shubert show *Blossom Time*. Besides the legitimate productions, vaudeville is drawing crowds at the State, the Hipp, the Empire, the Bandbox and the Majestic and especially the Palace! The format for the Palace is strictly vaudeville until 1926, and the **headliners who appear on the gigantic stage are the best: Fanny Brice, Jack Benny, Harry Houdini, Sophie Tucker, Ina Claire and Clara Kimball Young** among them. On May 23, 1926 the Palace switches to vaudeville and moving pictures, with continuous performances from noon to 11 p.m.

A night downtown on Playhouse Square might also include dinner at Monaco's in the front of the Hanna Building, the Lotus Garden Restaurant at 18th and Euclid or the Martinique on Huron. Nightclubs such as the Golden Pheasant and Henry's Chinese Restaurant feature entertainment figures like Rudy Vallee and Red Nickels and his Five Pennies.

Euclid Avenue is no longer the fashionable address for Cleveland's millionaires. The towering elms are gone, the street is paved and the mansions are disappearing one by one. But the Twenties bring a different kind of prominence to the main street. Theater lights, lines of people, elegant shops to rival those of New York's Fifth Avenue and ritzy dining spots make Euclid Avenue (and, particularly, Playhouse Square) the locale for the city's greatest activity and excitement.

The 1921 Euclid Avenue Association annual report makes these comments about the transformation of the street:

"...A generation ago Euclid Avenue was regarded as one of the most beautiful and dignified residential streets of the country. Now that it is not only the main traffic artery of Cleveland, but its main business street, it is a matter of pride to the city that it shall become as famous as a handsome commercial street as it was a street of homes. Within so short a period as the last 10 years, the character of the Avenue in different sections has changed beyond belief. It depends upon the guidance of public opinion, whether or not these changes shall be for better or worse."

But the effect of the decade's changes will soon be determined by something far more serious than "public opinion." For underlying these boom years is an air of desperation, and the pendulum eventually swings too far. In 1929, the stock market crash ushers in the lean years...

THE 1930s

During the early part of this decade, the contrast between poor and rich in America becomes sharply etched. It is estimated that one of every three Clevelanders is on relief during the depression years, and many are reduced to the humiliation of soup lines. On the other hand, the pursuit of pleasure continues for the wealthy, although entertainment activities do become more genteel than during the crazy Twenties. The speakeasies are turned into chic supper clubs which feature "swing" bands and popular singers. Cleveland proves to be a hothouse for musicians. Austin Wylie's popular dance band at the Golden Pheasant on Prospect has Vaughn Monroe and Artie Shaw among its musicians, and **Guy Lombardo often plays at the Music Box,**

Above: Crowds outside the Palace Theatre, 1929. Below: The bar of the Mayfair Casino (former Ohio Theatre Lobby), 1935-36.

Above: Mayfair Casino 'Sky Bar'
(former Ohio Theater balcony).
Below: Mayfair Casino, former
Ohio Theatre auditorium, 1935-36.
Inset: Mayfair Casino Program.

which is in the upstairs of the Loew's Building.

Representative of the elegant clubs of the 30s in Cleveland is the Mayfair Casino, which opens in the Ohio Theatre in 1935. The interior is completely redone in art deco with a huge mirrored circular lobby bar, tiers of tables filling the auditorium and a newly built circular stage for entertainment. Large crowds gather outside the Casino to watch the expensively-dressed celebrities arrive, but the glamour is short-lived and the Mayfair Casino goes bankrupt in November of 1936.

It is really the more inexpensive entertainments which flourish during the Thirties. This is the decade of radio, and families stay home during the week to listen to Amos 'n Andy, Burns and Allen, and Orson Welles' Mercury Theatre. And on Saturdays - well, on Saturdays, even millions of poverty-stricken Americans scrape together 25 cents to go to the movies. Over 85 million people a week flock to escapist fare like Busby Berkley spectaculars, Marx Brothers comedies and the new "family movies" featuring child stars like Shirley Temple and Mickey Rooney.

The big vaudeville houses in Playhouse Square now offer movies continuously with their live shows. And instead of vaudeville, personal appearances by names like Rooney and Garland are the popular draws at the State and Palace.

The apex of downtown movie entertainment for the decade comes in 1939 with the opening of *Gone With the Wind,* and Clevelanders form lines outside the Stillman Theatre for this blockbuster.

By now Cleveland is getting back on its feet. The real turning point for the city has come in 1936 with the opening of the magnificent Great Lakes Exposition, which occupies more than two square miles along the

lakefront. It is hoped that the Exposition will aid in the city's reconstruction, and it does foster greater business activity, employment, and best of all, enthusiasm. The Great Lakes Exposition includes a seven-acre Streets of the World exhibit, a 12-million dollar collection of art masterpieces, beautiful Horticultural Gardens, a midway with barkers, and a fireworks display to close each day's events. The Exposition remains open through 1937 and focuses nationwide attention on Cleveland. But while the city and the nation are recovering economic stability, a world crisis of monumental proportions is threatening. Once again a new decade will usher in a complete change in the temperament of the country.

Above: The Billy Rose show (á la Busby Berkley) in the Exposition's Aquacade. Right: Crowds outside the Stillman Theatre at East 12th & Euclid Avenue.

Top: Euclid Avenue at
East 2nd St., c. 1945.
Below: War bonds being
sold in State Theatre
Lobby, c. 1940s.

THE 1940s

... are the war years, and the world conflict infiltrates every aspect of American life, including entertainment. Hollywood begins turning out war movies by the dozens (largely romanticized, of course!). Theaters like the State become the sites for war bond drives, and movie stars tour the country to promote the sale of the bonds.

With the men away at war, women work on the home front, along with the young boys and girls. The 40's see the development of a cult of adolescent. American entertainment flavored by "juke box Saturday night," the conformity of fads and the rise of such "bobby sox" idols as Frank Sinatra. The popular fare in Cleveland and across the nation are movies, personal appearances by stars and big bands. **Even the "Voice" (Sinatra) comes to Cleveland to appear at the Palace.**

The post-War years inspire a rash of movies about our re-adjustment period, and interestingly, a renaissance in theater. Serious dramas by Tennessee Williams and Arthur Miller receive recognition, and this is also a bright epoch for the American musical theater. The spirit of entertainment activity is evident in Cleveland. You can take in a play uptown at the Play House or Karamu House or downtown at the Hanna. If you are spending the evening on Playhouse Square, you can see a movie and a stage show, with dinner before or after, and perhaps dancing. Highlighting the popularity of the area is the 1947 celebration of the Palace Theatre's silver jubilee, featuring a big stage show with Danny Kaye.

Above: Frank Sinatra. Below: Lines outside the State Theatre for Mickey Rooney, 1940.

Clockwise from top left: Danny Kaye lights the candles on Palace Theatre's 25th birthday cake, baked at Kaase's Bakery on Cleveland's west side, 1947. Judy Garland, Ziegfield Follies, 1945. Bob Hope. Fred Astaire. Mickey Rooney signing autographs for fans, c. 1940.

A Saturday night in downtown Cleveland is still something special during the 40's, but the pessimistic 50's will alter the city's nightlife considerably.

Above: RKO Palace Theatre marquee, 1946.
Right: Loew's State Theatre marquee, 1949.

Above: Cinerama at the Palace Theatre, 1958. Below: Palace Cinerama tickets.

THE 1950s

These are the jittery years. After the Korean War the nation becomes obsessed with Communism, subversion and The Bomb. The doomsday spirit inspires massive moves to the suburbs away from city life, and the development of a mass culture.

This is the era of "stay-at-home" entertainment. Television is the new American toy, with comedies, quiz shows and spectaculars mesmerizing the public. Popular novels are also zooming in sales, as people stay home in droves. In consequence, both the quality and quantity of theater and the output of the film industry are affected. Movie houses are closing all over the country, and those that remain open tend to show longer runs of epic movies.

During the early 50s, the Palace in Cleveland

becomes a Cinerama theater. Vaudeville is finally and irrevocably dead. Legitimate theater plays it safe, producing mostly big, popular shows like *My Fair Lady* and *Music Man*. The dominance of narrow, "safe" values is demonstrable in the popular idols, particularly the female stars. Even at opposite ends of the spectrum, Marilyn Monroe and Doris Day are light years removed from independent women of the 30s and 40s like Katherine Hepburn, Bette Davis and Rosalind Russell.

During the 50s adolescent interests will create an entirely separate mass culture, antithetical to the stuffiness of the older generation, but no less conformist in nature. Actors like James Dean, the sensitive rebel, inspire huge cults, which idolize the heroism of a delinquent way of life. Rock music replaces pop music in popularity and sets the tone for the confusion of the era.

It is significant that the arts do not die during the 50s; rather, they go underground. An intellectual elite reads novels by "beat generation" writers like Jack Kerouac, laughs at the cerebral humor of Mort Sahl and Nichols & May, and goes to see foreign films (especially as a result of the decline of the American film industry). The demands of this intellectual minority also gives rise to the "off-Broadway" movement as a reaction to the mediocrity of Broadway fare. But it is not until the decade of the keyed-up 60s that the "egghead" influences American tastes in a much broader way.

Above: Picketers in front of B.F. Keith's 105th St. Theatre, 1953. Right: Marilyn Monroe, c. 1950s. Below right: Film display in Ohio Theatre Box Office Lobby, 1944.

Above: Ohio Theatre
auditorium repainted red
after fire damage in 1964,
and later abandoned,
early 1970s.

THE 1960s

A nationwide acceptance of a new commitment to responsibility and a general spirit of optimism pervade the early 60s. John F. Kennedy's election to the presidency seems to lift the nation from the doldrums of the 50s. The arts are among the first areas to feel the effect of the vivacity of the Kennedy years, and middle-class America is suddenly more accepting of intellectual values. Young people become culture conscious, politically conscious, and, generally, more enthusiastically involved in the issues of the day.

But the shocking assassination of our president in 1963 kills the early optimism of the decade as well. And indeed, the late 60s seem to be characterized by violence, anonymity and a nationwide paranoia. In reaction to the well-publicized crises of the 60s, the frightened suburbanite more than ever avoids the necessity of coming downtown, particularly at night.

In Cleveland, the darkening of four Playhouse Square theaters becomes an apt metaphor for the mood of the nation. The closings occur, one by one, despite some last ditch attempts to "modernize" the venues. The Allen is completely redecorated and new wide-screen and stereo equipment installed in 1961, but the theater closes on May 7, 1968. The State is modified for Cinerama in 1967 by removing boxes and portions of marble railing. It is a desperation measure, for the State and the Ohio both close during the first week of February in 1969. Finally, the Palace Theatre closes on July 20, 1969 after its air conditioning breaks down during a showing of *Krakatoa, East of Java.* Of the five theaters remaining on Playhouse Square only the Hanna remains open for productions of road shows.

After the closing of the Palace, the marquee is torn down and its front boarded up. The sight is a depressing illustration of the decay of a once-thriving boulevard. Ironically, this final blow to the grand old theater prevents the Palace from becoming prey to vandals as are the Ohio, State and Allen. Vandalism, of course, is only a small element in the destruction of the theater interiors.

The Ohio has suffered extensive damage from fire earlier during the Sixties and the interior is completely covered with red paint in the "redecoration" after the fire. Most of the decor in the State auditorium is damaged or painted over with purple paint. Backstage areas of the Palace are in complete disrepair from years of neglect, and over the years treasures which once enhanced the interior have been sold. In both the State and the Ohio most of the seats are ripped out and sold at auction at the theatre closings. Chandeliers and other fixtures are sold. A mural above the mantel in the State auditorium is ripped off the wall. And while the theaters lie empty, holes in the roofs result in further plaster damage from rain and snow.

Few people in the community foresee the reopening of the theaters. The cost of the repairs and renovation work is not the only deterrent. Seating capacities of the theaters are now impractical for movie houses. Suburban shopping centers are building small twin cinemas or splitting larger houses. The movie-goer

Above: Palace Theatre marquee, July 1969.
Below: The mural in the State Theatre auditorium was ripped off the wall.

can now opt for convenience, especially since a night downtown no longer seems the exciting occurrence it once was.

Small wonder that old downtown movie palaces all over the country are being called "white elephants"… as if no one can perceive the importance of their existence as part of our architectural heritage and the possibility of adapting the structures to uses that are feasible today … as if no one can see the feasibility of saving our dying cities, let alone a building or two.

And yet at some point during the early 70s, cities across the nation begin to recover composure, reject the paranoia of the last two decades, and marshal forces to revitalize their downtown areas. In Cleveland, slowly but surely, a spirit of revivification seems to take hold. At Playhouse Square, in particular, a plan evolves not only for the preservation and restoration of four old theaters but also for the adaptation of the four existing structures into a complete fine arts and entertainment center. **The Playhouse Square Association comes into being.**

Removal of the Loew's State sign above the State Theatre marquee in 1972 marked the end of an era.

TRIVIA

A bomb exploded in front of the Hanna Theatre in 1971, shattering the marquee as well as the theater and Hanna Building windows. Placed to protest the production of "Hair" at the venue, the bomb caused $1,300 in damages. Two earlier threats had prompted the evacuation of the theater.

ENTER PLAYHOUSE SQUARE ASSOCIATION

FEBRUARY 5, 1970

ON THE 49TH ANNIVERSARY of the opening of the State Theatre, Ray Shepardson, an employee of the Cleveland Board of Education investigates the possibility of using one of the darkened theaters as a meeting place for teachers. Three weeks after his "discovery", *Life* Magazine features the Loew's State "Spirit of Cinema" mural on the fold-out cover of the February 27, 1970 issue. On the heels of this national attention comes a *Plain Dealer* article about the planned multimillion dollar renovation of Pittsburgh's Penn Theatre.

The chain of events is enough impetus for community leaders to begin

Above: Allen Theatre Marquee, November, 1971. Below: The Budapest Symphony Orchestra at the Allen Theatre.

Above: Allen Theatre's open ellipse at back of auditorium's main floor, c.1971.

plans for the "Playhouse Square Association," an organization which exists for a time only as an idea, its initial activities consisting of pleas to the community for support. But by July of 1970 Playhouse Square Association is formalized as a non-profit organization with a membership program. Lifetime members pay $120 with the proceeds used to begin shaping the plans for the four theaters. The first successful attempt by the Association to bring some activity to Playhouse Square comes during the fall of 1971. Plans are made to use the Allen Theatre for "special events" – an experiment to see if Clevelanders will actually come downtown for entertainment. On Sunday evening, November 21, 1971, the Playhouse Square Association presents its first event in the Allen – a concert by the Budapest Symphony Orchestra.

The performance is the first Cleveland appearance by the orchestra, one of Europe's top-ranking ensembles. Despite cold and windy weather, 2800 people (a sold-out house) attend the performance – proof positive that audiences will attend downtown entertainment events of quality.

Not only is the Budapest Symphony Orchestra concert a sell-out and an artistic success, it also results in a major surge of publicity for the Association: Pre-concert coverage, society page photos, favorable reviews from the music critics, editorials praising the efforts of the Association, and grateful letters to the editor. It is only the first of many such occurrences for the Playhouse Square Association. Newspaper, television and radio personnel, it is found, will go out of their way to support that which is positive, that which is beneficial to the city.

The second attraction presented by the PSA is a series of performances in December of 1971 by the Sierra Leone National Dance Co. As a special promotion, children are admitted free with their parents.

From January to May of 1972, sixteen more presentations draw crowds to the Allen Theatre for a completely varied selection of cultural and entertainment events. Among the Allen productions are: a showing of Czechoslovakian director Jan Kadar's film *Adrift;* a sold-out concert by British actor-singer Richard Harris; a special event for senior citizens featuring fan dancer Sally Rand; and a superb one-woman show by comedienne Lily Tomlin.

By March of 1972, things are looking brighter for the Playhouse Square Association. Over 400 people have become charter members, the upcoming Richard Harris concert is a sell-out, and *The Plain Dealer* features a full-page article about the Association's master plan to create an entertainment and cultural arts complex out of the four theaters. At this time, the plan is as follows:

• The Allen would house a cluster of small movie theaters without destroying the unique architecture of the interior.

• The State Theatre would be converted into a supper club-restaurant-nightclub complex.

• The Ohio Theatre would be a 1200-seat house for dance, theater, and chamber music.

• The grand Palace would be used as a 3500-seat concert hall for major events: opera, symphony orchestras, visiting dance companies, special theatrical productions.

More and more people are becoming convinced

Top left: Lily Tomlin.
Top right: Richard Harris.
Below left: Fan dancer
Sally Rand c. 1937.
Below right: Sally Rand
in a return visit to the
Palace Theatre in 1972.

THE PLAIN DEALER

WEATHER
Mostly sunny and warm.
High around 70; low in
the lower 50s. Chance of
rain is only 10%.
Details on Page 3-B.

COMPLETE
STOCKS
Dow-Jones up 3.16
RACE RESULTS

OHIO'S LARGEST NEWSPAPER
CLEVELAND, THURSDAY, MAY 25, 1972

131ST YEAR—NO. 143

★ ★

104 PAGES   10 CENTS

Loew's Ohio and State Theaters to Be Razed

By William F. Miller

The vacant Loew's Ohio and Loew's State theaters on Cleveland's Playhouse Square will be razed to make way for a giant parking lot.

Michael L. Miller, co-owner of Millcap Corp., told The Plain Dealer yesterday that bids were being taken for demolishing the building at 1515 Euclid Avenue that houses both theaters.

Meanwhile, Miller said, negotiations are continuing with the Playhouse Square Association, an organization trying to preserve the two former movie theaters and the nearby Allen and Palace theaters. The Allen now is open only for special events.

"WE JUST CAN'T go on forever keeping those buildings empty," Miller said.

"We'd like to do something to save them, but nothing has happened."

Miller said parking use would be the first step toward eventual development of new buildings for retail and entertainment use.

Miller and his partner, Benjamin F. Cappadora, recently purchased a 75% interest in the property from the Halle Bros. Co., giving them full ownership, according to Chisholm Halle, president of Halle's.

Halle declined to disclose the sale price. The department store, now a division of Marshall Field & Co., Chicago, acquired the property nearly three years ago to protect the Playhouse Square area for future development, Halle said.

"IT'S NOW A HORRIBLE eyesore,"

Halle said. "I see the demolition and future development as a positive move for everybody's benefit."

Halle said the Playhouse Square Association has done much to focus attention on problems of the area, and bring some activity there by reopening the Allen Theater.

Ray K. Shepardson, association director, said a "crisis situation" had been reached.

Unless Clevelanders come forward with the money to implement his organization's entertainment complex plan, the State and Ohio theaters are doomed, he said.

Shepardson's group, made up of some 400 members, is attempting to preserve all

Continued on Page 17, Col. 3

The Loew's Ohio and State theaters in Playhouse Square.
Plain Dealer Photo (Marvin M. Greene)

Above: Plain Dealer headline
from May 25, 1972.

TRIVIA

Thomas Lamb designed over 300 theaters during his career, thanks to his profitable business relationship with theater magnate **Marcus Loew**. With the lavishly designed Loew's theater empire covering half the country, Loew's motto was, "We sell tickets to theaters, not movies."

A design highlight of Lamb's theaters were the magnificent lobbies. Two of the grandest of the grand were side by side in Cleveland: Loew's State and (the "original") Ohio lobbies. Lamb's design appears to be the opulent gallery of Francis I in the sixteenth-century palace at Fontainbleau in France. The lobbies resemble that gallery in their decorative patterns, as well as their grandeur, which featured walnut wainscoting and a rich mixture of large murals and smaller paintings.

that Cleveland might actually create a complex comparable in quality and flexibility to the Kennedy Center in Washington, D. C. and Lincoln Center in New York City, but one which would be characterized by the unique qualities of each separate theater component.

And yet, despite bright outlooks and optimism, at this juncture a shoestring budget financed by membership dues and donations has just barely kept the project alive.

Then on May 25, 1972, disheartening news. *The Plain Dealer* headlines: "Loew's Ohio and State Theatres to be Razed". It is announced that the owners of the Loew's Building plan to demolish the building (which houses both theaters) in order to make room for a giant parking lot. The situation takes on a truly theatrical tone, with enraged editorials and letters to the editor, a 30-day reprieve for the Association from the City Planning Commission, and, dramatically, a pledge from The Junior League of Cleveland of $25,000 to help save the theaters does more to galvanize community leaders to action than the previous two years of hard work.

The groundwork laid by the Association leads to the formation of the Playhouse Square Operating Company in November of 1972 and Playhouse Square Associates in February of 1973, both to serve as channels of professional and financial support for the struggling

Association. The Playhouse Square Association itself maintains its purpose of working on the restoration of the theaters and promoting entertainment and cultural activities in the available spaces.

The first plan to be put into effect is the creation of a cabaret theater in the lobby of the State. The Association has spotted a musical revue entitled *Jacques Brel is Alive and Well and Living in Paris* at Cleveland State University and has decided to give the show a three-week run in the new Playhouse Square Cabaret. Under Joseph J. Garry, Jr.'s direction, the original Cleveland cast (Cliff Bemis, David 0. Frazier, Providence Hollander and Theresa Piteo) opens the new cabaret theatre April 18, 1973. The audience reception accorded the show turns a projected three-week run into a two-year marathon of bravos and record breaking celebrations.

September 15, 1973 ... BREL's 100th performance; October 31, 1973 ... BREL becomes Cleveland's longest running show ever; April 18, 1974 ... BREL celebrates its first anniversary; May 12 and 13, 1974 ... the BREL cast cuts the "Cleveland cast album"; February 19, 1975 ... the 100,000th customer walks through the Cabaret doors; April 18th, 1975 ... the second anniversary for BREL, and the show is selling heavily. Finally, on June 29th, 1975, *Jacques Brel is Alive and Well and Living in Paris* closes with a special performance. Over 800 BREL fans (many of whom have been to see the show 30 and 40 times) pack the Cabaret for an emotional farewell.

The BREL phenomena may be the greatest theatrical accomplishment the Association will achieve in terms of its box office success, but it serves also as the impetus for other productions. In the fall of 1973, monies from the Junior League make possible enough renovation work in the Palace Theatre to open a Cole Porter revue in the Grand Hall. On November 5, 1973, the opening of the new show and the 51st birthday of the Palace Theatre are celebrated with a gala benefit for Playhouse Square Association. *Ben Bagley's Decline and Fall of the Entire World as Seen Through the Eyes of Cole Porter* continues to run for over six months, closing in May of 1974.

Above: State Theatre Grand Lobby set up as a cabaret theatre during run of "Jacques Brel is Alive and Well and Living in Paris." Below: 1973 Jacques Brel program.

Above: "Cast of Ben Bagley's Decline and Fall of the Entire World as Seen Through the Eyes of Cole Porter," performs in the Palace Grand Hall, 1974. Below: A scene from "Alice!"

Fall of 1974 sees another opening and another kind of accomplishment – the presentation of a brand new musical by the Playhouse Square Association. *Alice!*, based on Lewis Carroll's *Alice in Wonderland*, is a collaboration by Playhouse Square Association artistic director Joseph J. Garry, Jr. and composers David Gooding (musical director for the Association) and Sy Johnson. The show, which stars Yolande Bavan as Alice, draws families with the Association policy of admitting children free when accompanied by adults.

Thus far only the lobbies of the State and Palace theaters have been used by PSA for theatrical productions, since the theater auditoriums need new seating and technical facilities as well as restoration work. The interior of the Ohio Theatre is almost totally destroyed. But the Association has not attempted to completely renovate the theaters before bringing the public in to see them. The point in making the theaters as accessible as possible to the public is to demonstrate their conditions upon their closings, alongside the progressing restoration work.

Currently the State is the theater which serves as the

most dramatic illustration of change. So in the spring of 1975 the auditorium of the State is transformed into a "tacky" nightclub for Fran Soeder's production of *El Grande de Coca-Cola*. This hilarious comedy revue opens in "El Club Grande" on May 9, 1975 to rave reviews; and large crowds come again to the State Theatre to enjoy a laugh-filled evening and to see restoration artist Rick Trela's work-in-progress.

This is a very satisfying period of activity for the Association. Overflow crowds jam the Cabaret for BREL's final performances. On weekends, people line E. 17th Street to see *Coca-Cola* as the show consistently begins to sell out. In addition, each week the State auditorium shows the increasingly dramatic results of restoration labors. Meanwhile, plans for the summer are rapidly falling into place. To replace BREL in the Cabaret on July 19th – a world premiere, *Conversations with an Irish Rascal,* a musical biography of Brendan Behan, adapted by Kathleen Kennedy with David 0. Frazier and starring Mr. Frazier and Irish folk singer Gusti. The opening of *Conversations* for a limited engagement is another step in the Association's plan to present new works in the available theater spaces as often as possible and, when feasible, to create new spaces for exciting and innovative work.

July also marks the month of an important fund-raising event for the Playhouse Square Foundation, a nonprofit organization founded to receive and administer charitable funds for the purpose of preserving art and architecture and supporting arts-oriented activities in the Playhouse Square area. On July 12 and 13, award-winning composer Marvin Hamlisch donates his time and talents to the Foundation in two concerts for the benefit of the Playhouse Square theaters. Hamlisch is the winner of three Academy Awards for *The Way We Were* and *The Sting* and, recently, winner of four Grammy Awards (including "Best New Artist of the Year"). He comes to Cleveland on the crest of another enormous success as musical composer for the New York hit show *A Chorus Line,* which has won the New York Drama Critics Circle Award for Best Musical of 1975.

Meanwhile, the bright new look of the Playhouse

Top: La Familia Hernandez from "El Grande de Coca-Cola." Above: State Theatre auditorium during run of El Grande Coca-Cola, 1975. Left: Composer Marvin Hamlisch.

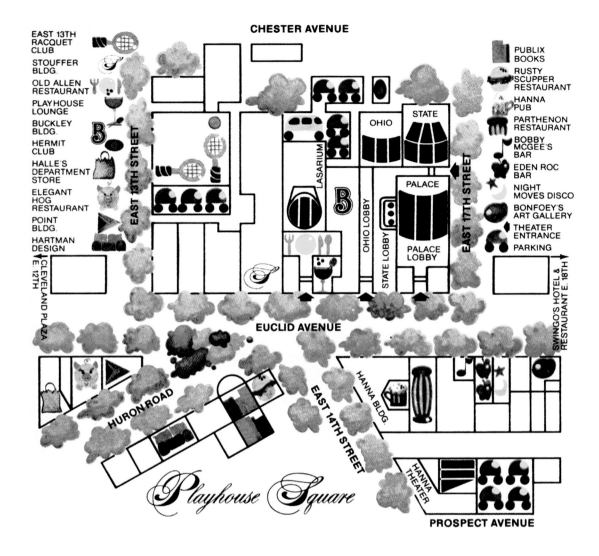

CHESTER AVENUE

EAST 13TH RACQUET CLUB

STOUFFER BLDG.

OLD ALLEN RESTAURANT

PLAYHOUSE LOUNGE

BUCKLEY BLDG.

HERMIT CLUB

HALLE'S DEPARTMENT STORE

ELEGANT HOG RESTAURANT

POINT BLDG.

HARTMAN DESIGN

EAST 13TH STREET

CLEVELAND PLAZA E. 12TH

LASARIUM

OHIO

STATE

OHIO LOBBY

PALACE

STATE LOBBY

PALACE LOBBY

EAST 17TH STREET

PUBLIX BOOKS

RUSTY SCUPPER RESTAURANT

HANNA PUB

PARTHENON RESTAURANT

BOBBY MCGEE'S BAR

EDEN ROC BAR

NIGHT MOVES DISCO

BONFOEY'S ART GALLERY

THEATER ENTRANCE

PARKING

SWINGO'S HOTEL & RESTAURANT E. 18TH

EUCLID AVENUE

HURON ROAD

EAST 14TH STREET

HANNA BLDG.

HANNA THEATER

Playhouse Square

PROSPECT AVENUE

Above: Map of Playhouse Square in the mid-1970s. Below: The Keg & Quarter at East 18th and Euclid Avenue.

Square area finds Clevelanders patronizing merchants like Publix Book Mart and dining in restaurants that include the Rusty Scupper, 'til Forbid and the Elegant Hog Saloon prior to their nights out at the theater.

While the city can boast the internationally renowned Cleveland Orchestra, the Cleveland Play House, Karamu House, and several beautiful museums; there are yet enormous gaps in the cultural life of the city. With funding for the necessary tech-renovation, the Palace can house the season of touring dance troupes, orchestras, opera companies, and special events that have disappeared from Cleveland over the last few years. In addition, the Playhouse Square Association anticipates that new resident companies can be housed in both the Palace and the Ohio.

The proximity of the Cleveland Dance Center, of Cleveland State University (which is eager to cooperate in artistic endeavors on Playhouse Square), and of businesses such as the Keg and Quarter (which has been extremely supportive of the Playhouse Square Association) are important factors in the growing impetus of the project. Thus are the efforts made in the area blessed with the status of "urban renewal." But what is happening here goes beyond commercial or even civic categorization.

Already the Cleveland Dance Center, with the support of the Cleveland Ballet Guild (a non-profit organization), has started work on the formation of a professional resident ballet company for Cleveland. Under the artistic direction of Ian Horvath, who was a soloist with the American Ballet Theatre; Dennis Nahat, formerly principal dancer and resident choreographer with American Ballet Theatre as well as choreographer for several Broadway shows; and Charles Nicoll, teacher and choreographer who has been responsible for the training of many professional dancers, the Cleveland Ballet will premiere its first full season in 1976, hopefully in one of the Playhouse Square theatrers. Currently the Dance Center is teaching classes (available for academic credit at Cleveland State University) in the Stouffer Building on Playhouse Square; with Horvath, Nahat, Nicoll and Pamela Pribisco as faculty. The Center is also training apprentices for its company and already has presented several preview performances. The Cleveland Ballet has the potential of bringing important attention to Cleveland at a time when American dance companies, both old and new, are receiving well deserved recognition.

The primary goal is, of course, the restoration of the Playhouse Square theaters. As buildings, these are objects worthy of preservation, yet they are not art objects in a static sense. Thus the Playhouse Square Association goals broaden to include the filling of the theater spaces with creative activities appropriate to their elegance, their intrinsic drama, imbuing the theaters once again with life. The heart of the Playhouse Square project is within the people who have committed themselves to these goals. They are people who feel a love for buildings that contain the handiwork of past generations. People who will sit in dark theaters simply to feel the ghosts surround them. Performers who have spent lifetimes, training for the moment of magic, the tran-

Above: Halle's Department store and the Point Building at the intersection of Euclid Avenue and Huron Road. Left: Detail of the Walker & Weeks "Mile Marker" in front of the Point Building. Below: Publix Book Mart.

scendence of reality. And people who come to see mirrored in those performers a facet of the soul that is not easily expressed in our daily existences. These are the people who "create" Playhouse Square and, in the words of the Edward Kleban – Marvin Hamlisch song from *A Chorus Line,* "won't regret what we did for love."

The other part of the battle, of course, is renovating

the theaters ... restoring the Ohio, State and Palace to their former splendor and creating a one-of-a-kind entertainment complex in the heart of downtown Cleveland. To this end, the Associates retain Peter van Dijk, nationally-recognized Cleveland-based architect acclaimed for his design of Blossom Music Center. His assignment ... to design a master plan for redevelopment of the theaters and the Playhouse Square district while preserving the rich architectural history of a bygone era. The work begins in late 1975.

In 1976, major internal organizational changes take place with the hope of strengthening the Association's ability to raise funds, restore the theaters and give new life to the Playhouse Square. The Playhouse Square Operating Company is merged into Playhouse Square Foundation; the Foundation is designated responsible agent for the management and redevelopment of the theaters; the Foundation Board of Trustees is enlarged from four to twelve members; a full-time Executive Director is hired.

Opposite page top: State Theatre auditorium dome, c. 1975. Below left: Promenade on mezzanine level of State Theatre, c. 1975. Below right: Detail from State Theatre's main floor ceiling at entry from Grand Hall.

This page above: The performer's view of the Palace Theatre stage.

TRIVIA

Amenities to the original backstage performer's area in the Palace included: a beauty/barber shop, billiard room, and putting green. Below the stage was a laundry room, tailor shop, sewing room and animal room. The animal room had tiled facilities to house, groom, and exercise various animal acts that were an intregral part of vaudeville.

Left to right: Mel Torme, Della Reese, Mary Travers, Chubby Checker, Bill Cosby, Bernadette Peters, Sarah Vaughan. Top right: Cast of "All Nite Strut."

1976 ~ 1977

Playhouse Square is still successfully experimenting with programming. In the fall of 1976, *All Night Strut,* a musical revue featuring four singers crooning tunes of the 1940s, opens in the State Theatre. Sponsored in cooperation with *The Cleveland Press, Strut* is the first of several Free Theater productions. The gamble pays off... the offer of free admission brings a deluge of ticket requests. The State auditorium is again hoppin' and *All Night Strut* becomes the second Playhouse Square production to go on tour following a successful Cleveland engagement.

Encouraged by the success of *Strut,* the Foundation in 1977 embarks on its first attempt to bring Las Vegas-style, big-name entertainment to Cleveland. Gracing the State stage are such names as Della Reese... Mary Travers ... Mel Torme ... Sarah Vaughan ... even the Houston Grand Symphony Orchestra with *Porgy and Bess* ... Bill Cosby ... Sergio Mendes ... Buck Owens ... Jack Jones ... Bernadette Peters ... Buddy Rich ... Fats Domino ... Chubby Checker.

Cleveland audiences, hungry for showbiz glamour that has bypassed Cleveland for too long, eagerly applaud and support the Foundation's efforts. The result... 289 concert-style performances attract more than 250,000 people.

But theatrical disaster still looms. The owners of the Loew's Building once again threaten demolition of the State and Ohio Theatres to make way for a parking lot. Playhouse Square Foundation, realizing the potential of the theaters as a community-wide resource, turns to the Cuyahoga County commissioners for advice and assistance in stabilizing the theaters' future and once-again halting the wrecking ball.

In December, 1977, discussions culminate in an 11th hour purchase of the Loew's Building by Cuyahoga County for $635,000. The theaters once again are saved! The Foundation signs a 40-year lease agreement with the county for management and restoration of the Ohio and State Theatres and the county appropriates $1.1 million to renovate the building's offices for county use.

This same month, the Foundation secures a long-term lease of the Palace Theatre, part of the Keith Office building, from private owners. **The three most important theaters in Playhouse Square are, for the first time, under single management and restoration authority!**

1978

In 1978, name entertainment programming moves to the Palace while the Foundation seeks funds to renovate the State and Ohio. Another programming experiment is undertaken – big-name talent at very-low prices. In cooperation with Revco Discount Drug Centers, a *Festival of Stars* brings to the Palace stage the talents of Kenny Rogers ... Pearl Bailey ... Doc Severinsen ... magician

Harry Blackstone ... Lola Falana ... Mel Tillis ... Red Skelton ... Marcel Marceau ... the Moscow Philharmonic. The *Festival of Stars* receives a thunderous welcome ... and audiences total more than 500,000 people!

The Playhouse Square theaters are listed in the National Register of Historic Places by the United States Department of the Interior in October, 1978. Meanwhile, the city of Cleveland allocates a $3.147 million Economic Development Administration public works grant to Cuyahoga County for renovation of the State Theatre audi-

Left to right: Lola Falana, Red Skelton, Doc Severinson, Marcel Marceau, and Kenny Rogers.

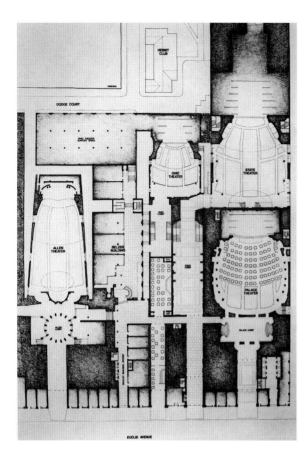

Above: Schematic drawing
of the 1979 Master Plan
for Redevelopment of
Playhouse Square, by
Dalton, van Dijk, Johnson
and Partners, Architects.

torium. A major breakthrough, this federal windfall provides solid reason to believe, for the first time, that the State
Theatre renovation and expansion will be accomplished.

A Cleveland Foundation-sponsored long-range
planning process begun last year reveals that five of six
local performing organizations will need new facilities
within the next five years. These five organizations, joined
by Playhouse Square Foundation, form a Cleveland
Performing Arts Consortium and successfully apply to the
National Endowment for the Arts for a $30,000 facilities
planning grant, matched by the Cleveland Foundation.

The groups retain Roger Morgan, nationally recognized theater consultant, and Christopher Jaffe, world-
acclaimed acoustician, to work with Peter van Dijk, lead
architect, to analyze the suitability of Playhouse Square
theaters for long-term use by the performing groups
needing a home.

The studies suggest that the State Theatre,
although shallow in stage depth, possesses properties of
auditorium size, acoustics and sight lines which make it
promising for opera, ballet and orchestra. Ironically, the
presence of surface-level parking to the rear of its stagehouse suggests a new stagehouse and support structure
can be built with relative ease using those lots. The Ohio
Theatre, although badly deteriorated, can be made suit-
able for classical theater, such as Shakespeare,

The $30,000 Design Arts grant from the National
Endowment for the Arts, matched by the Cleveland
Foundation, kicks off architectural planning for the most
efficient renovation, restoration and new construction of
the theaters.

The master plan for redevelopment of the theaters
as a performing arts and entertainment center is defined,
redefined, bounced off opinion leaders throughout the
community, revised and retested throughout 1979. A concept for raising funds, with probable sources and timeta-
bles, is developed. Changes in current operations are
instituted. Professionals, politicians, corporations, foundations, community groups, businesses, labor and local,
county and state government are all coming together with
Playhouse Square Foundation, demonstrating collective

will to create a major downtown entertainment resource which can be the product of an honest public-private partnership.

1979

In April, American City Corporation presents a proposal for Playhouse Square redevelopment to Cleveland business leaders, a redevelopment study funded by the Cleveland Foundation, Gund Foundation and Greater Cleveland Growth Association. In May, at long last, renovation begins in the State Theatre auditorium.

And in October, 1979, the best news of all ... the National Endowment for the Arts awards a $500,000 Challenge Grant to Playhouse Square Foundation. Clearly the years of hard work by a small, but visionary group of people are beginning to be recognized and rewarded as the Playhouse Square dream takes shape.

1980

March 4, 1980 the refurbished State Theatre marquee lights up Euclid Avenue as Playhouse Square Foundation announces an $18 million fund drive to complete renovation of the Palace, State, and Ohio Theatres to become a major new performing arts and entertainment center to

Above: "Stompin' at the State" set in the Grand Hall of the State Theatre, 1981.

service the broad Midwest region. Together the theaters will seat 7400 people and are expected to attract more than one million patrons each year.

In effect, the Foundation is saying to the Greater Cleveland community, "The experiment is over. This is what is required to complete a performing arts and entertainment center in Cleveland. If the center is important to the Cleveland community, if the center is to happen, the entire community has to work with us." At this point, not one dime is committed to the drive, except the NEA challenge grant.

Slowly and carefully, the community accepts the challenge. A steering committee is formed to oversee the capital fund drive. The mayor of Cleveland, president of City Council and the three County Commissioners agree that Playhouse Square should have top priority for any new federal funding for the city.

By summer, Phase One of the capital fund drive is underway. Major gifts include $710,000 from the Cleveland Foundation, $500,000 from The Standard Oil Company (Ohio), $500,000 from the George Gund Foundation, $300,000 from TRW Foundation, Inc. and

$200,000 from Eaton Corporation. In total, some $2.105 million is committed within the first six months.

In addition, Prescott, Ball and Turben, the largest Cleveland-based stock brokerage, announces its intention to purchase and renovate the abandoned Bonwit Teller Building in Playhouse Square as its national corporate headquarters. Hopes are high that other major real estate acquisitions and investments, dormant for many years, will swiftly follow.

Throughout most of 1980, the theaters are dark... reflecting the Foundation's plan not to present entertainment events until renovation is complete.

But in November the plan is modified. The Foundation opens *Stompin' at the State* in the State Theatre lobby, a re-creation of a 1940s nightclub. Running weekends only, *Stompin'* proves to be both an artistic and financial success. More importantly, it enables the Foundation to keep the Playhouse Square name before the public while fundraising and renovation continue. *Stompin'* runs for 16 months, playing to more than 45,000 people.

The Foundation also is successful in bringing people back downtown for the holiday season. In December, 1980, and again in 1981, the Junior League of Cleveland presents its Holiday Festival of Trees in the State lobby, an event which attracts more than 10,000 people each year.

In 1981, a $3.5 million grant from the Economic Development Administration of the Department of Commerce – first promised by the Carter administration in 1980 then frozen earlier this year by the Reagan administration – is finally reinstated. Matched by a $3.5 million grant from Cuyahoga County, this completes the $7 million funding needed for the new State stagehouse. At the same time $1.25 million in Urban Development Action Grants also help finance the renovation of the Ohio Theatre.

By year-end 1981, more than $15 million is already committed to the Playhouse Square project, an accomplishment of truly stunning proportion. And restoration of the Ohio Theatre has begun. The most derelict and damaged of the three theaters and the most difficult to

Above and below:
A craftsman repairs damaged plaster along the proscenium of the Ohio Theatre stage, 1981.

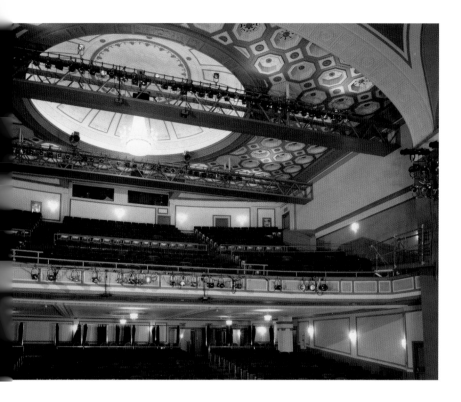

Above left: Ohio Theatre after renovation. Above right: Ohio Theatre chandelier. Below: Ohio Theatre before renovation in 1982.

reconstruct, the Ohio had been expected to be the last theater to be restored. However, the scenario changes when the Great Lakes Shakespeare Festival finds it needs a permanent new home in 1982. Discussions and analysis by Foundation and Festival officials during 1981 confirm that the Festival can be housed in the Ohio IF the theater can be readied for the Festival's 1982 22-week season.

Working at breathtaking speed, the architectural firm of Dalton, van Dijk, Johnson and Partners completes plans and drawings and Dunbar Construction Company performs complicated, state-of-the-art renovations.

JULY 9, 1982

The renovated Ohio Theatre opens its doors! The intimate, 1000-seat Ohio, with $4 million worth of restoration, is technically outstanding and fully accessible to the handicapped. It is completed in less than nine months at a cost savings to the community of some $14 million – the difference between the cost of renovating the Ohio and building a new theater, proposed earlier, along Lake Erie.

During the Ohio's first season, more than 130,000 people attend performances of the Great Lakes Shakespeare Festival, Cleveland Modern Dance Association, Ohio Chamber Orchestra, Ohio-Ballet, Slovene Folklore Institute, a Children's Theatre Series co-sponsored by PSF and the Junior League of Cleveland and touring artists. The Great Lakes Shakespeare Festival itself draws 77,500 people to its first season in downtown Cleveland. Among its attractions is the acclaimed *Nicholas Nickleby,* the first American performance of the 8 1/2 hour drama outside New York City and a production which focuses international attention on Playhouse Square.

Within its first year, the Ohio Theatre is already demonstrating what Foundation officials have predicted right along – that an array of smaller productions and theatrical companies, both local and national, need a downtown performing home in order to thrive and grow and that people from the entire Northern Ohio region will come to the heart of Cleveland for entertainment they can't find anywhere else.

By year end 1982, the capital fund drive reaches nearly $16 million and Phase One is concluded. But the timetable for completion of the center is pushed back, from two years to four years, because of delays in acquisition and Federal funding for the State Theatre stagehouse.

Restoration of the Palace Theatre dressing room towers, a $600,000 combined project of Diamond Shamrock Corp., the Junior League of Cleveland, Inc., The Northern Ohio Design community and construction

Above: Great Lakes Shakespeare Festival's production of "Nicholas Nickleby." Below: "Renaissance" Playbill for GLSF's Annual Fundraising event.

OHIO THEATRE

RENAISSANCE

The Great Lakes Shakespeare Festival

Saturday, June 26, 1982

T R I V I A

The Ohio's Grand Lobby chandeliers were acquired from the Erlanger Theatre in Philadelphia, PA, and the current chandelier which hangs in the Ohio's main auditorium comes from Cleveland's old Hippodrome Theatre. (Its twin hangs in the main dome of the Palace Theatre in Columbus.)

Above left: Palace Theatre dressing room, 1922. Above right: Palace Theatre dressing rooms before renovation. Below: Palace Theatre dressing rooms after renovation.

trades, is completed in April and serves as The Junior League's Decorator Showhouse in 1982. The twin towers, with 20,000 square feet of dressing rooms and office space, are lavishly restored, decorated and furnished for public viewing. From April 25 through June 6, more than 20,000 people tour the towers.

In 1982 the City of Cleveland and the Foundation commission two important studies, both vital to the long-term development of the Playhouse Square area. Halcyon Ltd., a Hartford-based nationally-recognized mixed use developer of urban real estate, is retained to analyze the economic development and marketing potential of the Bulkley Building Complex, adjacent to the theaters. The second study, by Kaczmar Architects, Inc. of Cleveland, focuses on traffic patterns, parking needs, building conditions in the district and a community development plan.

The Halcyon study in particular, proves to be key. In July, 1982, the Cleveland Foundation, for the benefit of Playhouse Square Foundation, purchases the Bulkley Building complex adjacent to the theaters. It is the first time in the nation that a community foundation has invested its assets, not its income, in a geographic area where it already has a significant charitable stake.

The complex is of central importance in the long-term development of the Playhouse Square district. The purchase assures the availability of the complex for future development.

The re-opening of the Ohio Theatre ... the successful completion of the Phase One capital fund drive ... acquisition of the Bulkley complex... such monumental events are cause for celebration! The Foundation does so in grand style September 11, 1982 with a gigantic block party, co-sponsored with the city of Cleveland and Greater Cleveland Growth Association. Continuous entertainment from morning till midnight, displays, food and fun bring more than 25,000 people to the Center.

MARCH 18, 1983

Construction begins on the new $7 million State Theatre stagehouse! At a groundbreaking ceremony, a wrecking ball whacks the soon-to-be-replaced back wall of the State ... and years of waiting, planning, hoping and coping with delays and stumbling blocks finally come to an end. The proper completion of the second gem in this three-gem crown has finally begun!

Phase Two of the capital fund drive is launched in June, 1983. At its helm are three prominent Greater Clevelanders: Roy H. Holdt, Chairman of the Board and Chief Executive Officer of White Consolidated Industries, Inc., Edwin M. Roth, Chairman of APCOA and the Electronic Theatre Restaurant Corp., and Diann G. Scaravilli, civic leader and past president of the Junior League.

Within months, generous support is received ... $1.7 million from businesses ... $870,000 from foundations. 1983 also tests a variety of entertainment... preparing, in miniature, for the array of offerings available when all three theaters are open.

Experimental live jazz in Kennedy's five nights a week in the summer... *Broadway Babies*, a musical revue on weekends ... extended three months.

Inset: Palace Theatre proscenium medallion. Below: A scene from "Broadway Babies," staged in Kennedy's.

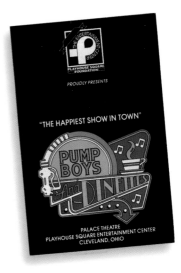

Pump Boys and Dinettes opens for a one month run at the Palace in October, 1983 and is extended for four months. After 121 performances, some 51,476 people have seen and loved the show.

Another 30,000 people come downtown in a four-week period, again to the Palace, for *Little Shop of Horrors*, an award-winning wacky musical about a people-eating plant. Performed by the national touring company, the Cleveland visit is the first stop in a year-long *Little Shop* tour and rehearses here … signaling the growing national reputation of the Playhouse Square Center as a first-rate theatrical facility.

Dracula or a Pain in the Neck by the New Vic Theatre of London … the magic of Landis and Company… modern dancers … traditional ballerinas… excellent orchestras … joyous sounds of a chorus… an original musical *Chicken Little* produced, performed and staged by The Cleveland Magnet School of the Arts … even the return of films to Playhouse Square when the Cleveland International Film Festival sponsors Fassbinder's Berlin Alexanderplatz in the Ohio Theatre to a sellout crowd… all tell us that even before completion of the entertainment center, uncommon entertainment is bringing audiences and attention to Playhouse Square.

Above: "Pump Boys and Dinettes."
Below: "Little Shop of Horrors" poster, 1983.

JUNE 9, 1984

The curtain rises on the renovated State Theatre and its new $7 million stagehouse. The Playhouse Square Center, just a dream a few short years ago, is a reality!

The celebration takes many forms …

A gala party … music, dance, entertainment, food and festivities throughout the Ohio, State and Palace Theatres from early evening till the wee hours of the morning … and on the new State stage, a star-studded spectacular features Mike Douglas … Diahann Carroll … Roberta Flack … Les Ballets Trockadero de Monte Carlo … Michael Davis.

Gala guests arrive in style… walking up a red carpet to the State door past a welcoming committee of white-gloved Playhouse Square attendants. Outside … trumpets blare … video cameras whir and flashbulbs explode.

An opening festival… throughout the month of June, the celebration continues. Celebration Square to Square, in its third year, brings 100,000 people downtown for a gigantic block party … the Metropolitan Opera of New York celebrates its 100th anniversary with a week-long engagement at the State, its new home for annual spring

Above and below:
State Theatre
auditorium, June 1984.

visits … the Cleveland Orchestra performs in concert on the State stage … soul singer Aretha Franklin brings Mahalia, a tribute to gospel queen Mahalia Jackson, to the State for one week.

An inaugural season… features a stunning variety of entertainment … the Alvin Ailey American Dance Theater… Mazowsze, a Polish folk dance troupe… four world renowned orchestras, including the Royal Philharmonic conducted by Yehudi Menuhin … four Children's Theatre Series productions … The Kenley Players with Juliet Prowse, Tony Geary, John Davidson, Mitzi Gaynor… and more.

With one of the largest stages in the world, 65 feet deep… a stagehouse as tall as a 10-story building… sprung dance floors… two large rehearsal rooms… and countless other amenities, the State Theatre has doubled in size. It is now home to the Cleveland Ballet and Cleveland Opera and is capable of hosting world-class productions of every description.

Also opening in 1984 is Playhouse Square's new computer center to service the box office, finance, marketing and development departments. With seven windows opening onto the State lobby 35 phone lines and 30 computer terminals, the center embodies the centers professional scale and scope.

The Foundation's new IBM 36 computer prints tickets at the push of a button, facilitates sales of single tickets and subscriptions and constantly updates records, mailing lists, donor lists and financial data.And in 1984, the Foundation's capital fund races toward successful completion. By June, more than $23 million of its $27 million goal is already achieved… with victory very much in sight.

Playhouse Square Association has now joined Playhouse Square Foundation, as the Foundation's financial support arm, and the future development of the Playhouse Square district, beyond the theaters, has been consolidated under the Foundation. A master plan for Playhouse Square is being developed and several landmark buildings have been restored or renovated for new, useful lives. Others stand waiting in the wings.

Above: The "Met" loads into the new State Theatre Stagehouse. Below: Playbill and ticket from the Metropolitan Opera of New York's 60th Anniversary Tour at the State Theatre, 1984.

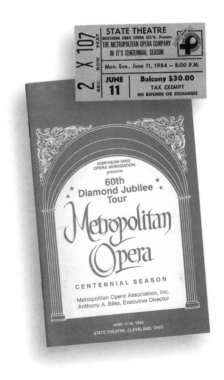

NEXT ACT...

THE PALACE THEATRE...THE BEAUTY of a venue hidden for generations under dust and crumbling plaster still waits in the wings for restoration to its former grandeur. A $3.75 million grant from the State of Ohio is in hand to begin the process.

This move to revive the Palace to its glory days expects work to commence in '84, continue on through '85 and culminate with the theater's grand reopening in 1988.

1985

Below: Palace Theatre Grand Hall, 1922.

March, 1985...an ambitious undertaking is afoot, as the Foundation launches its "Campaign to Complete Playhouse Square Center." The goal: to raise $12.4 million. This effort, in turn, draws unqualified support from

Above: Scene from
Cleveland Ballet's "The
Nutcracker," 1984.
Below: "The Nutcracker"
playbill, 1984.

Cleveland Tomorrow, an organization of CEOs from 40 top Cleveland companies. They make it their number one physical development priority, pledging to help finish the project.

Although the original plan had called for work to begin on the Palace restoration in 1985, the Foundation pushes back the start of renovation construction until funds are in hand to assure completion of the project. The amended goal? Commence construction in March, 1987, with completion slated for spring 1988.

While the wait for the Palace's renovation is frustrating, the Center can still bask in the limelight of its expanded performance schedule. Due to the success of a triumphant 1984 three-week holiday "Nutcracker" run, **the Cleveland Ballet announces that it (along with "The Nutcracker") has adopted the beautifully restored State Theatre as its permanent home.**

1985 also finds the State playing host to film luminaries Anthony Quinn (*Zorba*), Ann Miller and Mickey Rooney (*Sugar Babies*), as they take their turn on the boards of a venue which boasts a 65-foot stage... not to mention a spacious orchestra pit that can accommodate 85 musicians.

And when attractions such as the Minnesota Orchestra aren't appearing onstage, informal concerts (like those performed by the Ohio Chamber Orchestra) are conducted in the lobby. The State Theatre Lobby also substitutes as a grand baronial hall April 29th - May 4th for elegantly-dressed patrons of the Met's annual Opera Week. Gourmet pre-performance dinners and elaborate decor greet Met patrons, as Opera Week continues to reign as the highlight of Cleveland's social scene.

But when the Met departs, Cleveland's own Cleveland Opera readily fills the gap with a spectacular *Aida* and an inventive wild West setting of *The Elixir of Love.* The public response is so great that the company expands its 11th season, opening with sold-out performances of *The Merry Widow,* starring the Met's beloved Roberta Peters, dazzling in the title role.

In 1985 the Foundation dons yet another exciting new hat: producer and more visible presenter of artistic product. Both roles have splendid results. Ten years after its original triumph, *Brel* was back! *Jacques Brel Is Alive and Well and Living In Paris* had been the catalyst production that first brought people to an unrenovated Playhouse Square Center a decade earlier.

First performed in the *lobby* of the State Theatre for a record-holding 522 curtains, the returning *Brel* now takes the State *stage*. This welcome reunion features all the original cast members: Cliff Bemis, David Frazier, Providence Hollander and Theresa Piteo, plus musical director David Gooding and director Joe Garry, Jr. Once again, *Brel* is a hit! It entertains more than 20,000 people for 48 standing-ovation performances during a two-month revival.

Above: Scene from Cleveland Opera's production of "Aida," 1985. Below: Scene from Cleveland Opera's "The Merry Widow."

Above left: "Do Patent Leather
Shoes Really Reflect Up" herald,
1985. Above right: Great Lakes
Theater Festival's production of
"Arsenic and Old Lace"
starring Jean Stapleton, 1985.

Brel's launching of the Foundation's second season
proves to be the harbinger of a joyous year of stars, stars,
stars: Richard Harris in *Camelot,* Susan Anton and
Elizabeth Ashley in *A Coupla White Chicks Sitting Around
Talkin',* Jean Stapleton in Great Lakes Theater Festival's
Arsenic and Old Lace, Oscar-winning Estelle Parsons in
Miss Margarida's Way and Bolshoi expatriates Valentina
and Leonid Kozlov in *On Your Toes.* Also enjoying unpar-
alleled success this year is the comic run of *Do Black
Patent Leather Shoes Really Reflect Up?*

Meanwhile, back in the State's rehearsal room, a
new musical work-in-progress, *Diamond Studs,* is incubated, and – when fully produced – is scheduled for national tour. At the Center's intimate Kennedy's cabaret
space, PSC produces its own comedic parody to the play
Cats… this one naturally titled *Dawgs.*

At the Ohio Theatre, Great Lakes Theater
Festival and its new director, Gerald Freedman, take
bows for such memorable productions as *Twelfth Night.*

Throughout the year, the Cuyahoga Community

College-sponsored free series, "Showtime at High Noon", continues as a powerful people magnet, attracting patrons to the Center for this popular lecture-demonstration format that showcases all the arts.

Even the Cleveland Orchestra makes a sojourn from its home at Severance Hall for six State Theatre performances, musically celebrating *Film Classics* and *A Tribute to Duke Ellington*.

In addition to the burgeoning theatrical schedule, free monthly tours and national teleconferences draw audiences to the Center from some 40 states, the District of Columbia and Canada. The result is $10.5 million worth of tickets purchased and a cool $26.4 million for the coffers of Greater Cleveland via related entertainment expenditures such as lodging, dining, parking and shopping.

Elation over these new-found tourist dollars validate the Center's role as more than a mere local attraction. **It has become an important mecca for prestigious entertainment, helping to elevate Cleveland as a "destination" city**… and this is only the beginning.

By the close of 1985, the substantial impact of the Playhouse Square Center development is confirmed in a study by the Regional Economic Issues Program of the Federal Reserve Bank of Cleveland. Their analysis: "the Center is the catalyst for rising property values, rental rates and occupancies in surrounding buildings; significant increases in tax revenues for local governments, and a 22% increase in business located in Playhouse Square since 1983".

These independent findings herald significant implications for the Foundation as it continues to plan for the future of Playhouse Square Center and the theater district in general.

T R I V I A

The Ohio's lower-level intimate club setting, known as Kennedy's, features a bar that was formerly part of the Elegant Hog Saloon when the tavern was located on Buckeye Road.

Above: The Cleveland Orchestra poster presenting "Film Classics" and "A Tribute to Duke Ellington." Below: Merchandise displayed in The Prop Shop.

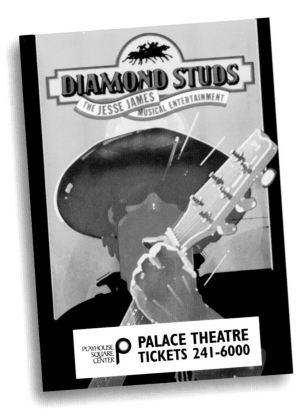

Above: "Diamond
Studs" playbill.

1986

1986 is to be a year of rave reviews and stellar financial news. The front page of the *Plain Dealer* breaks a story that has Playhouse Square smiles stretching from stage left to stage right. A $500,000 challenge grant is awarded to the Center from the Kresge Foundation of Troy, Michigan.

This generous gift is among the largest announced by that Foundation in 1986. But more important than the "size" of the gift is its "significance". Playhouse Square Center had been tenaciously applying for the grant on a regular basis since the Seventies. Its acquisition is synonymous with recognition: an independent, out-of-state funding source (the largest private financial supporter of capital projects in the United States no less) had awarded the grant based on the most considered analysis, weighing it against the appeals of hundreds of other worthy applicants. It is most definitely an endorsement of the Center thus far, and an encouragement to proceed with its ambitious plan for the future.

The euphoria doesn't even begin to settle when, the very next day, the Kresge grant news is followed by another important announcement. News comes by way of Washington, D. C., informing Playhouse Square that it can count on the addition of $2.6 million, courtesy of an Urban Development Action Grant.

Not to be outdone by the Federal government, the State of Ohio is next to step up to the financial plate. At a surprise news conference March 3rd, Governor Richard F. Celeste announces plans to appropriate $5 million in support of the Campaign to Complete Playhouse Square. By the fall of 1986 the Foundation is miraculously only $1 million shy of its $12.4 million goal!

Meanwhile, the day-to-day business of entertaining guests takes center stage. The Metropolitan Opera (although uncertain about its future) is resplendent in its 61st visit to Cleveland, as it entertains an elegantly gowned and tuxedoed audience.

Theatre League (which makes the Center its home for Broadway productions) offers up *Dreamgirls, The Tap Dance Kid, 42nd Street* and a splashy revival of *Singin' In The Rain,* complete with elaborate special effects that produce an actual rain shower on stage. Audiences love it!

Also on the theatrical horizon is a bold new step… the first incubation of a new musical, *Diamond Studs, The Jesse James Musical Entertainment,* a sassy celebration of folk history.

Diamond Studs will prove to be an historic moment for the Foundation. By incubating new plays away from the creative stress and financial pressure of New York, the dramatists, actors and directors are given a rare opportunity to shape ideas and sharpen their talents sans the high-anxiety and hustle-bustle of Broadway.

At the same time, this incubation process treats Cleveland audiences to fresh shows and faces (in advance of their Broadway peers) along with the sheer pleasure of being present for the birth of a new production.

Seventeen years earlier, the Palace had closed with little hope for the future. Now, even in its unrestored state, the grand old venue is enjoying limited activity while awaiting its major overhaul. Government and corporate organizations as well as private citizens are dedicating their efforts to save the Palace from the fate that closed so many downtown theaters, plunging the former bustling district of 16 original venues into an entertainment ghost town.

If critics believed that the overwhelming success of the Center's inaugural season could be chalked up to novelty or nostalgia, the repeat business and record-breaking totals of fiscal 1986 proves that the "product" deserves the credit.

The comedy *Do Patent Leather Shoes Really Reflect Up?* boasts 136 performances, **selling more tickets here in Cleveland than it ever had during seven previous years**, which included runs in major markets like New York, Chicago, Boston and Philadelphia. In December alone, the Center attracts more theatregoers and more dollars than in *any* previous month in its history!

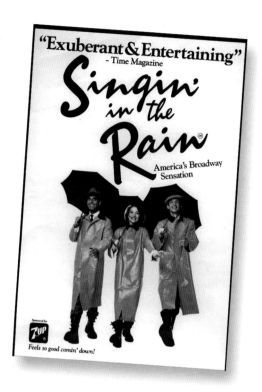

Above: Playbill from the Theatre League's revival of "Singin' in the Rain." Below: Palace Theatre auditorium awaits restoration.

1987

Across the board in 1987, the entertainment choices become kaleidoscopic for PSC ticket buyers, including **the national premiere night grandeur of the Michael J. Fox Cleveland-filmed movie** *Light of Day,* to legendary mime artist Marcel Marceau, who captivates a standing-room-only State Theatre crowd.

All previous box office records are broken with The Theatre League of Cleveland's presentation of the feline phenom *Cats.* The synthesis of high-tech and high-touch sells 7,608 tickets to *Cats* in just one day... one every seven seconds! Center volunteers serve hot coffee to hundreds of *Cats* buyers who have braved a long line that snakes out into the blustery winter weather.

The Center's production of *Pump Boys and Dinettes* draws capacity crowds to a special return engagement in Cleveland, and *Big River,* the Huck Finn musical, is co-produced by PSF for a blockbuster week of performances. Donning its producer's hat once more, the Center spearheads a nostalgic look at the music of the '50s & '60s via the national tour of *Beehive,* which buzzes its way into an instant sensation.

Meanwhile, PSC constituents are busy with a host of attractions, including an impressive coup by Great Lakes Theatre Festival in the form of Mr. George Abbott, the dean of Broadway showmen. Abbott directs GLTF'S revival of two of his best-loved works – the musical comedy *The Boys From Syracuse* and the melodrama *Classic Broadway.* During the run of these signature productions, **GLTF and PSC are proud to help Abbott celebrate his 100th birthday!**

World-renowned prima ballerina Cynthia Gregory graces the Cleveland Ballet as guest artist for the '86-'87 season, and **for the first time at the Center, Cleveland Ballet performs the aesthetically visual and artistic *Swan Lake.***

DANCECleveland audiences also revel in the electrifying style of the company's co-presentation of The Alvin Ailey American Dance Theatre, plus The Twyla Tharp Dance Company and *Pilobolus,* long a favorite of modern dance enthusiasts.

Above: Playhouse Square 'lights up' for the premiere of "Light of Day," starring Michael J. Fox. Below: Michael J. Fox arrives at the State Theatre.

Entertainment aside, the key word for 1987 is still "construction" with a capital "C". **The State Theatre's three lobbies are totally refurbished in an amazing six months** at a cost of $1.2 million, and ground is broken in May to construct a new PSC parking garage. Completion of the parking facility is hoped to coincide with the opening of the Palace.

In the Founder's Lobby, crystal plaques are hung bearing the permanently-etched names of people and corporations whose major gifts had halted the wrecking ball before it could knock the heart out of this piece of Cleveland's history. **(The skillful artisan of these plaques is none other than Lucas "Larry" Century, the Cleveland native responsible for the engraving of the Vietnam Memorial in Washington, D.C.)**

Palace Theatre renovation begins in January, following the six relentless years it took to secure the needed $36.4 million. When the dollars are tallied at the close of the Campaign to Complete Playhouse Square, the figure is over the top...$37.7 million raised! Cleveland once again shows its charitable colors.

Now for the elbow grease. **Craftsmen are in place to work their magic with the three "R's": restore, repaint and regild.** The masterful and ornate plasterwork featured on the walls and ceiling is repaired and, in some places, recreated before being painted and gilded in the fashion of its artisan predecessors.

The proscenium arch and sought-after side boxes (destroyed in 1956 when Cinerama was installed) are rebuilt with the aid of old photos. Craftsmen carefully cast molds of existing sections of the arch to accurately recreate the original.

Also on the repair list is a 140-foot section of iron and brass staircase railing, a 20-foot by 10-foot brass door, and sundry other hardware pieces throughout the theater. Another major project will involve replacing the entire orchestra floor and reterracing the balcony to improve sight lines to the stage.

Modern technology works its wizardry with the outdated heating, electrical and plumbing systems. State-of-the-art lighting and sound is installed with a special

Above: Playbill from GLTF's revival of "Classic Broadway," directed by George Abbott. Below: The new Founder's Lobby of the State Theatre.

Above: The Palace Theatre's side boxes
are rebuilt during 1987-88 renovation.
Below: The Palace Theatre's side boxes
were removed in 1956 to accomodate
a "cinerama" screen.

acoustical wall to prevent sound "bleed" from the Palace
to the State. A dramatic scenario sees a helicopter lower
the new air conditioning unit onto the State lobby roof.

In the stage area, a hydraulic lift enables the orchestra pit to be lowered from sight, then replaced with additional seating when an orchestra is not required. Quality
supercedes quantity, with larger seats and wider aisles
reducing the seating from 3500 to 2800, in order to provide guests a greater comfort zone.

**In the "good news" category comes disclosure that
the cost to renovate Playhouse Square's three venues is
roughly half of what other communities are spending to
construct just one new theater!**

TRIVIA

When it opened in 1922, the original art collection that
decorated the Palace was valued at a half-million dollars. Oil
paintings hung on the walls of the Grand Hall and around the
promenade level. They were later sold at auction after WWII.

Above: The Palace Theatre Grand
Hall after 1988 restoration. Left:
Palace Theatre auditorium, stage and
orchestra pit under construction.
Below: A craftsman repairs one of
the Palace's many chandeliers.

Above: Newly renovated Palace Theatre Auditorium, 1988. Left: Burt Bacharach and Dionne Warwick headline the Gala entertainment. Below: State and Local Civic Leaders join Playhouse Square President, Lawrence Wilker and Trustees in a Ribbon Cutting Ceremony.

1988

It is a project of heroic proportions: hundreds of workers... artisans, architects, engineers, theater designers, acousticians, brass restorers, sophisticated millworkers, restoration painters, rigging and lighting experts, plumbers, electricians and concrete workers... all pooling their collective talents during 12 months of construction. These gifted craftsmen gloriously complete the Palace restoration. They bring the project home not only on time, but – miraculously – on budget.

The much-anticipated Palace Theatre grand reopening on April 30th is heralded by *The Plain Dealer* **as "one of the great Lazarus acts in America." Its opening night benefit gala nets approximately $500,000... the largest sum raised by a single benefit to that point in Cleveland history!**

Gala-goers are as captivated by their first look at this lavish example of Cleveland's architectural history, as were their grandparents at the theater's original opening back on November 6, 1922. Then, as now, the theater's

name is indeed apropos...a "Palace" designed in the French Imperial style.

The grandeur of enormous crystal chandeliers (reminiscent of the Palace of Versailles), plus intricate Old World ironwork, valuable Sevres porcelain and magnificent sweeping twin marble staircases dazzle and impress.

Inside the theater, singer Dionne Warwick and composer Burt Bacharach headline the gala entertainment, along with the music of Tex Beneke (who, two generations earlier, had appeared at the Palace with the famous Glenn Miller orchestra). Outside, theater-goers are greeted not only by a new Palace marquee, but an impressive sign rising five stories high heralding "PLAY-HOUSE SQUARE CENTER" in lights.

Critics who had questioned the need for yet a third restored theater in the Center's complex, would now comprehend the reasoning behind the decision to renovate the Palace:

Along with other regular users, the State and Ohio

Above: Palace Theatre Grand Lobby after renovation is complete, 1998. Below: A 'full house' awaits the curtains to rise on the Palace Theatre stage.

Left to right:
Whoopi Goldberg,
Basia, Kenny G. and
The Pointer Sisters.

venues were occupied much of the year by the Center's non-profit resident companies, making dates scarce for the availability of worldclass touring ensembles. The Palace was the logical alternative site to house these touring shows, as well as providing a venue for the Center's germinating plan to book many of its own attractions.

With the completion of the Palace, a programming void could now be filled by new genres previously missing from the Center's entertainment mix. This programming expansion and flexibility will appeal to a wider audience, further validating the Foundation's goal to serve the tastes of the entire populace. The Palace availability also expands producing opportunities, allowing the Center to incubate, workshop and develop new and neglected works of American musical theater.

(As a result of this opportunity, the Center mounts a critically-acclaimed production of *The Gospel At Colonus*, a retelling of the ancient Greek myth in the setting of a present-day Pentecostal church. The show moves on to Broadway for a three-month engagement, becoming a Tony Award nominee.)

The Palace availability also provides the opportunity for PSC to forge new partnerships in the industry, allowing other promoters to bring in acts from various entertainment genres.

Added to 1988's $8.25 million Palace restoration is an $8.2 million parking garage, soon to feature a heated-and-cooled glass connector to provide even more convenience for Center guests, while it also serves the daytime neighboring office population.

The PSC entertainment scene continues to prosper, with Broadway entries such as *The Music Man* with John Davidson, *Me and My Girl*, *Can-Can* and the sensuous rhythms of *Tango Argentina*.

Showbusiness youngsters like Kenny G., comedienne Whoopi Goldberg and singer Basia are joined by contemporary artists Air Supply, Robert Palmer, Linda Ronstadt and The Pointer Sisters, while veteran talents Rosemary Clooney, Steve Lawrence & Eydie Gorme, Jackie Mason and Mitzi Gaynor continue to pack 'em in.

In addition to *The Marriage of Figaro* and the World

Premiere of *The Legend of Sleepy Hollow*, Cleveland Opera is the first opera company in the Western Hemisphere to receive the rights to present *West Side Story* with the original Jerome Robbins choreography, not seen in Cleveland since the 1950s.

With three theaters currently restored, the Foundation could have been content to rest on its successful laurels. Nothing is farther from the truth. Now begins a scrutiny of the entire theater district, initiating an ambitious plan to revive the area to its former glory. Agreements are reached for a new $32 million small luxury hotel and a planned $40 million, 250,000 square-foot class-A office building, complete with attached 400-car parking structure. These are to be constructed on land owned by the Foundation, which will be sold to developers. This project signals a milestone: the first new construction at Playhouse Square in over 50 years.

1989

Playhouse Square Center's fiscal year ending June 30, 1989 is the litmus test for all previous optimistic assumptions. **For the first time in anyone's memory, all three theaters are fully restored, up and running for a full 12 months.** It is the most demanding yet exhilarating time in the Center's 14-year history. The numbers alone give a sense of excitement, with over 700,000 people pouring in from 49 states and 11 countries to see some 700 events.

Broadway offerings include: illustrious ladies Carol Channing and Mary Martin in *Legends,* Topol in *Fiddler on the Roof, Into The Woods, Steel Magnolias, Driving Miss Daisy, Nunsense,* and – the talk of the season – *Starlight Express* with its roller coaster choreography.

Left to right:
Bonnie Raitt, Loretta
Lynn, Dolly Parton,
Anne Murray and
Lou Reed.

As theatrical landlord, the Foundation continues to host six resident companies which bring brilliant diversity to the stages of the Center ... an artistic bounty enabled in part by a subsidy provided by the Center's under-cost rents.

Yet another demographic is attracted to the Center thanks to Cleveland International Film Festival's hosting of **the world premiere for the film** *Major League.* A red-carpeted arrival of the stars is covered by all Cleveland media, who delight in the fact that the victorious heroes in the movie are none other than Cleveland's own Indians baseball team.

The Center receives additional international recognition and artistic acclaim when Cleveland Opera unveils the new production *Holy Blood and Crescent Moon* by Stewart Copeland, former drummer for the rock band Police. **Since the Center is the site for this world premiere of Copeland's work, it attracts international press coverage ranging from conservative daily newspapers and trade publications to rock music magazines.** In addition to the premiere of the Copeland work, Cleveland Opera also presents the Cleveland premiere of *The Pearl Fishers.*

The rest of the music world is well represented throughout the year: Dolly Parton, songbird sisters Loretta Lynn and Crystal Gayle, Anne Murray, and Bonnie Raitt, Lou Reed, plus those artists headed for induction into the Rock and Roll Hall of Fame and Museum: Bob Dylan, Frankie Valli & The Four Seasons and The Four Tops.

Stand-up comic newcomers, Sinbad and Steven Wright, are joined on the PSC laugh track by *The Living Legends of Comedy* trio of Danny Thomas, Milton Berle and Sid Caesar.

Another comic legend, Red Skelton, relates this interesting story from his last Palace Theatre booking ... 50 years ago!

Skelton was an impoverished vaudevillian who was told by the Palace manager, "Kid, you got talent. Why don't you go to Hollywood and take a screen test?" Red said, "Because I barely have bus fare home." The Palace manager reached into his pocket,

loaned Red the train fare to Hollywood, and, inadvertently, launched the career of one of comedy's brightest stars.

The Palace plays host to what is hoped will become an annual international folk festival. The rich history of ethnic entertainment dates back to the 1922 opening night of the Palace, with a performance by Spanish dancers, The Cansinos.

(The forerunner of this latest International Festival traces its roots to *All Nationality Week* featured at the Palace in 1926. Groups of performers, each representing a specific nationality, were showcased on succeeding nights: Sunday... Irish Night; Monday... German Night; Tuesday... Welsh, Scottish, British Night; Wednesday... Italian, French Night; Thursday ... Hungarian, Roumanian Night; Friday... Spanish, Swiss, Czechoslovakian Night; and Saturday... All-American Night.)

Playhouse Square is now in the third year of its "incubation program." Half a dozen shows are under development including *Eating Raoul, The Apprenticeship of Duddy Kravitz, Big Man, The Secret Garden* and *Theda Bara.* Ultimately, the goal of the Center is to revive the endangered musical theater art form to help satisfy America's hunger for original works. With each successive project, Playhouse Square Center's fame (and Cleveland's) grows as a viable workshop location, hospitable to major talent.

Beyond the walls of the Center, the Foundation continues to receive recognition in a variety of forms. Requests by outside companies for national consulting assistance is on the upswing, including work with the New York State Development Corporation on a project involving 10 theaters on New York City's 42nd Street. Ditto for the Los Angeles Historic Theater Foundation which requests help in the development of 10 theaters in that city's downtown area.

Back at home, the Center becomes a driving force in Theater District development, **as the first major building to rise in Playhouse Square since the 1920s is a direct result of the Foundation's efforts.** The $40 million Renaissance Office Building adds a post-modern profile

Above: "The Living Legends of Comedy" trio of Danny Thomas, Milton Berle and Sid Caesar.

STAR NOTES

During his last visit to Playhouse Square Center, comedian **Red Skelton** insisted on personally shopping for his show props at a local K-Mart. Red's presence became the Blue Light Special of the day, as word spread through the store that the legendary Skelton was a fellow shopper. Red became so mobbed by fans that it took him two hours to check out. Leaving K-Mart he asked his limo driver to take him to his favorite lunch spot... Bob Evans Restaurant.

Above: The Renaissance Building at East 14th and Euclid Avenue. Below: Pre-Reinberger Lobby.

to the Theater District's skyline.

With the completion of the Renaissance Building, focus turns to the next Playhouse Square-initiated project: a luxury hotel to be built on the site of the old Point Building where Euclid Avenue, Ontario and E. 14th streets intersect. The Renaissance, in tandem with the hotel, will dramatically enhance the district's image, concurrently changing its economic dynamics.

1990

Plans are finalized and work begun on a dramatic new entrance to the Ohio Theatre's Gallery lobby. Made possible by a generous gift from The Reinberger Foundation, the completed lobby is reminiscent of a Florentine courtyard, featuring faux marble statues and a starry sky. **This "starred" effect is known as "atmospheric theatre", and is currently the only one of its kind in the Cleveland area.**

In June, a suite of tastefully renovated rooms off the Ohio Theatre lobby is dedicated as "The Patrick A. Sweeney Educational Center", honoring State Representative Sweeney, whose efforts over the years were vital to the success of the Playhouse Square Center project. The Sweeney Center will function as a downtown instructional facility and reception area for Cuyahoga Community College, which continues its pivotal role at PSC.

The Kirkham families, long-time advocates of Playhouse Square Center, dedicate the Ohio Theatre Auditorium in honor of their grandfather, Oscar M. Gilbert. The dedication recognizes the families' generosity throughout the years to the Center.

July celebrates the opening of the Renaissance Office Building, constructed on land owned by the Foundation. But with the celebration of one triumph, comes news of a setback. For the time being, the battle is lost to save the Allen Theatre because it sits on land that has never been owned nor controlled by the Foundation.

The Allen's current property owners are discussing demolition of the auditorium, with possible plans for a restaurant in the Allen's ornate lobby. However, the

Foundation continues to appeal to the owners that a restored Allen is more vital to the Center and the City than any alternative plan for the property.

This is the Foundation's second season of operating three fully-restored theaters. Attracting over 750,000 guests to the Center (a 20% gain over the previous year), **PSC continues its dual role: home for the arts – and – one of Cleveland's most effective urban redevelopment tools.**

An ever-widening spectrum of entertainment possibilities continues to draw new audiences to the Center with the inauguration of a Classical Festival, generously supported by The Cleveland Foundation and The John P. Murphy Foundation.

The Festival's performances include opera luminary

Above: Ohio
Theatre's Reinberger
Lobby, 1990.

TRIVIA

Stargazers take note. The eye-catching "atmospheric ceiling" in the Ohio's Reinberger Lobby features stars using fiber optics and a special effect machine created to project clouds. The only other Cleveland theater to feature an atmospheric ceiling was the now-demolished Granada Theatre on the West Side, which closed in 1970.

Above: The Canadian Brass. Below: Legendary "Show of Shows" comics Sid Caesar and his cohort Imogene Coca.

Kiri Te Kanawa, The Los Angeles Philharmonic and The Atlanta Symphony Orchestra. The Canadian Brass (in an anything-but-stuffy performance), delight audiences not only with their musical prowess, but by marching up and down the aisles decked out in tuxedos and... sneakers.

The resident companies also enjoy a distinguished year. Cleveland Opera marks season #15 with a pair of "Dons": *Don Giovanni* and *Don Pasquale*. GLTF celebrates its ninth season with *The Lady From Maxim's*, *La Ronde* and **... its brand new production of *A Christmas Carol*.**

With *Christmas Carol*, GLTF has a decided hit on its hands. Delighted audiences break all sales records, speculating that this success could herald an annual visit by the holiday production, much like Cleveland Ballet's *The Nutcracker*.

Distinguished conductor Andre Previn includes a PSC Cleveland stop as part of his farewell tour with the Los Angeles Philharmonic, while at the State Theatre, the unmistakable sound of the Mantovani Orchestra treats its audience to the brilliance and mastery that made the legendary conductor a household word.

Legendary *Show of Shows* comics Sid Caesar and his rubbery-faced cohort Imogene Coca offer a rare appearance, while their young comedy peers Howie Mandel, Elayne Boosler and Gary Shandling polish stand-up techniques for the MTV generation.

Broadway offerings present an interesting mix, ranging from *Peter Pan* and *The Unsinkable Molly Brown* to *Beauty Shop* and Juliet Prowse as the flamboyant *Mame*. **This marks the first year that Playhouse Square Center acts as its own manager of the Broadway Series, eschewing outside promoters.**

1991

Despite the difficulties posed by a local and national recession, the Foundation is still able to meet its operating goals, and, at the same time, make significant progress in other areas.

Meanwhile, a new program called Playhouse Square Partners is created to attract a young donor group. The Partners organization is designed for professionals who look to make new friends, network and become involved with a cause that also benefits their city.

Inside the Center, the Ohio Theatre auditorium and lobby are repainted in a style more in keeping with the Center's other theatrical spaces. The magnificent architectural detail of the auditorium is matched to the original designer's specifications.

Concurrently, outside the Center, the Foundation's real estate activities makes strides on two fronts: the sale of the land on which stands the Renaissance Office Building for $2.5 million, (monies which are des-

Above: Andre Previn and The Los Angeles Philharmonic.
Below: Ohio Theatre architectural details.

Above: Great Lakes Theater Festival production of 'Uncle Vanya" with Hal Holbrook. Below: Rudolf Nureyev and Cynthia Graham in rehearsal hall.

ignated for a future endowment fund); and progress on the hotel project. Trade union pension funds committed to finance half of the $12 million required for the project bring the specter of this planned luxury hotel one step closer.

Great Lakes Theater Festival kicks off the year January 5th with what is to be one of the season's highlights: a one-man show written and performed by the Festival's most famous alumnus, Oscar-winning actor Tom Hanks. GLTF continues to keep impressive company with the likes of Hal Holbrook and Robert Foxworth in *Uncle Vanya*, and Avery Brooks, as he creates a fiery portrait of the great Paul Robeson.

Cleveland Opera presents the performance that has all Cleveland talking: *Aida* is resplendent in a triumphal scene featuring live camels, monkeys, birds, a zebra and even an elephant, not to mention brilliant dances for the opera's production by the Cleveland Ballet.

"Triumph" likewise describes the '90-'91 season of the Cleveland Ballet and their European debut. Dancing with the company is international ballet legend Rudolf Nureyev (who performs in both Dennis Nahat's *Coppelia* and the company's premiere of *The Overcoat* at the Edinburgh Festival). Nureyev returns to the U.S. to open Cleveland Ballet's home season at the State. It becomes the must-see production of the year.

In November, the Center receives international press coverage. Rock and Roll Hall of Fame and Museum committee notables have gathered at the Ohio Theatre to make the annual announcement of the latest roster of Rock Hall of Fame inductees to the world media. This is the first time the induction announcement has been made from Cleveland – now home to the soon-to-be constructed Rock Hall and Museum.

Jerry Seinfeld, who is on the brink of becoming the hottest new star on the comedy horizon, appears, as does filmdom's Burt Reynolds in a rare speaking engagement

Program-wise, '91 is a daring success as *The Plain Dealer* co-sponsors a new *Festival of Stars* series, bringing to town Liza Minnelli, The Smothers Brothers, Andy Williams and Marilyn McCoo. Positive feedback on its premiere season convinces PSF to make *Festival of Stars* an annual subscription series.

Thanks to *Festival of Stars* and the Broadway series, 45% of the total revenues for fiscal 1991 are from Playhouse Square Foundation presentations. This has been a dramatic increase from 1990, when Foundation presentations accounted for only about 15% of ticket revenues.

Back patting is the order of the day when the Foundation learns that yet another Playhouse Square incubation, *The Secret Garden*, has won a Tony Award and is tagged by *Time* Magazine as "the best American Musical of the Broadway season". For this successful production, Playhouse Square Center is listed in the Broadway playbill as "Co-producer", lending even greater credibility to PSC as an important "player" in the creation of new Broadway product.

Meanwhile, the Cleveland Ballet launches its own stellar productions, including the premiere of Agnes DeMille's work, *Fall River Legend* and by popular demand, *Romeo and Juliet* returns.

1992

After five years of detailed paper work and innumerable setbacks, the Foundation finally closes in on the financing necessary to build the planned hotel project. This prudent, conservative investment will not only change the face of the Theatre District, but provide welcome accommodations to the million-plus visitors to Playhouse Square, not to mention the neighboring venues of Gateway's Ballpark and Arena, Cleveland State University's Convocation Center, the upcoming Rock and Roll Hall of Fame and Museum and Great Lakes Science Center.

The financial picture is rosey as well within the Center. For the fiscal year ending June 30, 1992, earned income contributes to 91% of total income. (Ticket sales alone represent over 60% of these earnings.) Also on the plus side of the ledger, 1992's gala, *Steppin' Out*, stars singer/songwriter Melissa Manchester and raises over $100,000 for the Foundation.

The year sees the Playhouse Square "Partners"

Above, left to right: Penn and Teller, Jerry Seinfeld, Liza Minnelli, The Smothers. Below: Playhouse Square Partners "Jump Back Ball," 1992.

The Kimball Organ

On February 2, 1992 the third theater organ to be placed in the Palace is dedicated. The three manual, thirteen rank Kimball, built in 1927 for the East Liberty Theatre in Pittsburgh was donated to Playhouse Square by Gary Brookins in 1975 and was painstakingly restored by volunteers, headed by Bill Tabor.

The 'new' Palace organ contains: 13 sets of pipes, a xylophone, Glockenspiel, celesta, a complete set of drums and many cymbals. These unique sounds enter the auditorium through lattice grills in the ceiling, on each side of the stage.

Below, left to right:
Peter, Paul and Mary,
Mandy Patinkin,
Tommy Tune,

organization grow from its founding nine members to over 300 in just two years. Together, they stage the first-ever PSC leap-year event, aptly tagged "The Jump-Back Ball". The party is such a success that the Partners vote to make it an annual February event.

The Center has become a virtual revolving door for the hottest contemporary acts in the business. Triple-talented musician/composer/recording artist Yanni holds his sold-out audience in rapture for over two hours, with a standing ovation that seems nearly as long. Ditto for the popular Mannheim Steamroller celebrating five sold out Christmas shows.

The Plain Dealer's second *Festival of Stars* season hosts Broadway's darling Mandy Patinkin, fireball Rita Moreno, the irrepressible Tommy Tune, England's famous duo of Cleo Laine and John Dankworth, and folk singing legends Peter, Paul & Mary.

(Mary Travers, of Peter, Paul & Mary, had been among the first acts to play the Palace when it re-opened in the Seventies. She became one of the stars to lend a volunteer hand to the painting restoration in the State Theatre, adding her brush strokes to history.)

PSC's continued incubation of new product germinates a number of success stories. The

Foundation's investment in *The Buddy Holly Story* is rewarded, as the show (with the Foundation as associate producer) proves a smash hit on the road, recouping 100% while still on tour. After a long Broadway run, another PSC incubated show, *Prelude to a Kiss*, is made into a movie.

Also on the incubator front, *Guys and Dolls* wins four Tony Awards, and its weekly sales breaks the Broadway records held by Andrew Lloyd Webber's *The Phantom of the Opera*. The tours of *Barnum* and *Forbidden Broadway* are likewise successful – and – *The Secret Garden* wins three Tony Awards then heads to PSC's Palace to triumphantly open its national tour, moving to the Jewish Repertory Theater in New York City.

The Foundation's co-production of *Song of Singapore* (begun here at the Ohio Theatre), finally closes in New York on June 30 after 481 performances... an extraordinarily healthy run! Currently in review by the Foundation are a number of shows, including a revival of *Tommy*, the musical stage version of The Who's classic rock opera from the late Sixties. Presently in "workshop", *Tommy's* first staging is expected to take place in the coming year at California's La Jolla Playhouse.

In 1992 Playhouse Square Center continues to host not only the creme de la creme of entertainment, but VIPs from the world of news and politics, as witnessed by the Town Hall sponsored speaking engagement of England's former Prime Minister Margaret Thatcher.

Above: Above: "The Secret Garden" on Palace Theatre stage, 1992. Below: Scene from "Song of Singapore."

1993

Mergers, missions and "music of the night" characterize 1993. This will be recorded as one of the most ambitious years in Playhouse Square's history since the commencement of renovation. It becomes both literally and figuratively a "groundbreaking" year for the Foundation.

Two long-negotiated events become catalysts to boost Playhouse Square's annual attendance past the one million mark. At a March 3rd press conference, PSC President Art J. Falco and Front Row Theatre Owner/ President Larry S. Dolin announce a merger between the

Above: The Front row Theatre closes its venue in 1993 and joins forces with PSC to bring more acts to the downtown theaters.

Center and the successful suburban Front Row venue.

With the imminent arrivals of a new arena, ball-park, science center and Rock Hall of Fame on the urban horizon, both Falco and Dolin look to downtown Cleveland as the coming mecca for area entertainment. They have the foresight and vision to realize the important role Playhouse Square Center will play in this entertainment mix.

As the 20-year-old Front Row closes the doors on its Highland Heights location July 1st, and moves operations to the Center, the consolidation is expected to result in over 100 added curtains each year for PSC, entertaining an additional 200,000 concert-goers.

The Front Row's booking infusion promises a higher profile for Playhouse Square in the genres of country, rhythm-and-blues, gospel, jazz, rock, comedy and adult contemporary acts.

Also making the move to Playhouse Square Center is Front Row's veteran "Dialogues" Speakers Series. Likewise for the Front Row Children's Theatre Series, which will complement the Foundation's existing "Discovery" youth series by attracting an even younger segment of children, from pre-kindergarten through grade three.

But as the Front Row's circular stage turns its final revolution, another theater is about to rise like the classic phoenix from its doomful ruins. The Foundation has scored yet another coup. Thanks to lengthy and non-defeatist negotiations, the Allen Theatre will, after all, be saved! A successful agreement has been reached with the Bulkley Building Partners for a long-term lease to sustain and operate the 72-year-old landmark venue.

The Allen has been part of the Foundation's renovation master plan since the early '70s, and this signing comes just in time to avert demolition of the historic structure. Dedicated fans of the Playhouse Square restoration project are elated that this final sibling in the quad of theaters will now join the family as a full-fledged venue.

Plans commence to evaluate the best use for the Allen's flexible space. Meanwhile, dedicated volun-

teers, from students and housewives to businessmen and even a congressman, rally to the cause, spending over 1000 hours cleaning the theater's musty interior. This massive effort enables PSF to utilize the Allen's impressive Rotunda for the annual Playhouse Square Center gala.

While the Allen was on the road back from being the phantom of the theater district, the phenomenon of another "phantom" makes history and changes lives over at the State Theatre.

Andrew Lloyd Webber's masterpiece, *The Phantom of the Opera* opens April 25th for an eight-week run, selling out every available seat to every single performance! (This includes 40 nightly standing-room-only positions, which boosts total attendance figures to an amazing 196,509 patrons.)

But the drama is hardly confined to the *Phantom* onstage: during one performance a pregnant patron goes into labor at intermission. Her husband asks for replacement tickets so they may return to see the show's conclusion. (He gets them.) On another evening, a

Above: Scene from "The Phantom of the Opera." Below: "Phantom" playbill.

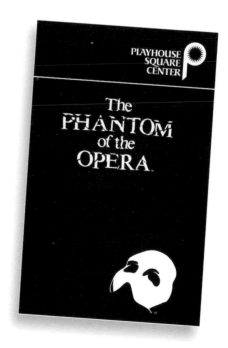

Above, left to right: PSC's "Dialogues" Speaker Series guests First Lady Barbara Bush, General Colin Powell, and opera diva Beverly Sills.
Below: Groundbreaking ceremonies for the planned luxury Wyndham Hotel.

child who has been virtually silent for years is so moved by *Phantom* he miraculously begins to weep and talk. It is a performance the child's parents will never forget.

The cast members of *Phantom* also exhibit a personal agenda to help change lives. They play one entire performance without pay to donate the show's revenues to AIDS research.

From as far away as Seattle and Miami patrons venture from 36 states and two Canadian provinces to experience *Phantom* in Cleveland. The "Phantom" run even attracts bus tours from Manhattan! The play's ticket revenues of $8.9 million translate into at least $20 million in total economic benefits for the city of Cleveland from related tourist dollars.

The resounding success of *Phantom* brings to the fore the underlying need to create more vibrancy in the environs surrounding the venues. In this vein, the Foundation issues a "request for proposal" to the nation's top urban design consultants to develop an exciting new look for Cleveland's theater district.

Response is immediate and enthusiastic. A panel of Cleveland architects, museum professionals, urban land specialists and Foundation executives review proposals, selecting the firm of Thompson and Wood. The firm will propose economically feasible ways for the district to enliven itself with restaurants and businesses, while retaining a unified theatrical flair.

The first of the Front Row Theatre cum Playhouse Square bookings premieres July 6th with New Orleans' favorite sons, The Neville Brothers. The former Front Row "Dialogues" series premieres at the Palace, hosting such high profile speakers as First Lady Barbara Bush and prosecutor Vincent Bugliosi from the Charles Manson trial.

1993 as a "groundbreaking" year takes on the translation literally when, in July, the mayor, local politicians, Playhouse Square trustees, executives and staff assemble at 14th and Euclid for the long-awaited ceremony that turns the first gold shovel of earth in a ground breaking for the planned luxury hotel (a co-development of PSF and Wyndham Hotels).

1994

Where "Broadway" is concerned, the most personal satisfaction for the Foundation climaxes with their co-production of The Who's *Tommy*. It is a production with which the Foundation has been involved since the show's incubation, so there is ample back-slapping as *Tommy* walks away with five Tony Awards, including Best Score and Best Choreographer.

The touching story of *Tommy* is the first Broadway show in anyone's memory to feature such a panoply of rock 'n' roll special pyrotechnics, including lasers, spinning Veri-lites, sparklers, fog and wind machines. While being de rigueur for the MTV generation, these effects are new to many veteran theatergoers.

Meanwhile, "standing room only" is the byword for the year's hottest comic, Jerry Seinfeld, who sells out his entire four-performance booking in a matter of hours!

PSC's "Dialogues" Speaker Series scores a decided booking coup: the most sought-after speaker of the year, Persian Gulf War hero, General Colin Powell (Ret.). A former Cleveland resident also participates in "Dialogues", as Emmy, Grammy and Presidential Medal of Freedom recipient and opera diva Beverly Sills opens the speaker series.

As Sills engagingly recounts her life in opera, Cleveland Opera sets new box office records, expanding its repertoire in both geography and style. Fairy tale sets and lavish costumes for *Cinderella* create a breathtaking family production, while Jerome Hines, in highlights from *Boris Godunov* in *A Russian Opera Gala*, is memorable in the title role. (Hines is famous for singing this quintessential Russian role at Moscow's Bolshoi.)

Great Lakes Theater Festival's season opens with the film and legit celebrity of Lynn Redgrave in *Shakespeare For My Father*, and culminates with a memorable staging of Arthur Miller's masterwork *Death of a Salesman*, featuring a stellar lcast ead by native Ohioan Hal Holbrook in his return to GLTF.

Within the Center, focus turns to the Allen Theatre, a venue successfully saved from the wrecking

Above: Scene from
"Tommy." Below:
"Tommy" playbill, 1994.

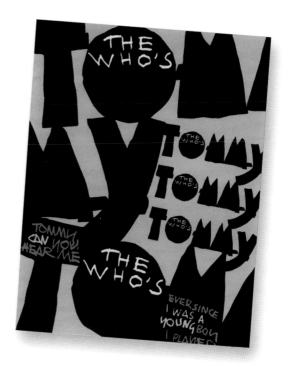

Above and below: Temporary staging, light bridges, and cabaret seating are installed in the Allen Theatre auditorium in preparation for the opening of "Forever Plaid" in Fall of 1994.

ball the previous year by the Foundation. But like the restoration sagas of the Palace, Ohio and State theaters, an up-to-speed Allen will hardly emerge overnight. Renovation presents the daunting requirements of complete replacement of hidden systems (like wiring, plumbing, heating and air conditioning), before craftsmen can even begin to work their aesthetic magic on the falling plaster and fading paint.

The Allen will be the last step in what Clevelanders may not realize is … **the largest theater restoration project in the world!** When the Allen is completed, Playhouse Square Center will rank **second only to New York City's Lincoln Center as North America's largest performing arts complex.**

In the short term, while capital funding can be raised, the Allen is cleaned and put to use for the type of small cabaret shows that play to great success in New York City, Boston and Chicago.

On November 9th the Allen becomes home to the light, witty musical production, *Forever Plaid*. What had been a dank ruin of a space only a year before, sees 60,000 people walk through its doors to be entertained by *Plaid*. Only the Allen's lack of air conditioning forces the production to halt for the summer. It returns in the fall, once again playing to capacity crowds, many of whose patrons are seeing *Plaid* for the third and fourth time!

1995

The "Dialogues" Speaker Series takes a comic turn with political satirist Mark Russell and National Public Radio's "Whad'ya Know" host Michael Feldman. But the '95 series "heavyweight" is veteran film star Gregory Peck, every bit the legend, as he enraptures fans with career memories and Hollywood insider stories before taking on audience questions. (One life-long fan is thrilled to

share with Peck the story of how her son came to be named after the screen idol.)

Cleveland-born comics Steve Harvey and Drew Carey (returning to their hometown hot off successful TV series), both sell out their PSC shows, with Carey sending his audience laughing into 1996 at his New Year's Eve performance.

In all, nearly one million theatergoers purchase tickets to see a record 777 performances in 1995. In the month of December alone, PSC entertains 133,047 people – or – 4900 per day (excluding Mondays, when the theaters are dark). **Ten short years ago it took as long as three months to host as many guests as the Center now serves in only one day!**

The Center's dramatic growth in audience has added urgency to the expansion of a Theater District where a symbiotic mix of nightlife and entertainment can thrive. Currently, PSC activity spins off over $60 million in

Above: Thompson & Wood, of Cambridge, Massachusetts, develop a Master Plan for Cleveland's Theater District in 1994, which includes graphic concepts to revitalize and add excitement to the urban landscape.

Below left: Gregory Peck.
Below right: Drew Carey

revenue to the community. With plans to incorporate more shops, restaurants and clubs into the district's long range plans, revenues will continue to rise.

Another District milestone is celebrated on July 7th. Workers, supporters and trustees gather to cheer as the ribbon is finally cut on the new $27 million Wyndham Hotel, owned, in part, by Playhouse Square Foundation. The District's theatrical theme is embraced by the hotel, which names its ballrooms and meeting salons for such classic Cleveland theaters as the Palace, Roxy and Hippodrome.

Above: The Wyndham Hotel at Playhouse Square prepares for its Grand Opening, July 1997. Left: Gregory Hines. Below: The Wyndham Hotel at Playhouse Square takes 'center stage' in July 1998.

PSF further celebrates the Wyndham opening with a "Grand Entrance Gala" on July 8th. Attendees get their first up-close look at the new hostelry and are treated to the fancy footwork of the evening's star, world-renowned dancer Gregory Hines.

The next construction spin-off is slated to be the creation of a public plaza in the triangular property fronting the Wyndham. Star Bank comes forward to sponsor this plaza, which receives contributions as well from the State of Ohio, the Garden Club of Greater Cleveland, the Shaker Lakes Garden Club and Cleveland's Bicentennial Commission. "Star Plaza" is envisioned as a creative mixture of a classic European park combined with special effect lighting, a glass gazebo and space for live entertainment.

As Playhouse Square Foundation carries the concept of public-private partnership to new heights for the area, the District is expected to set a contemporary standard for urban renewal, just as the PSC theaters have set the standard for historic theater renovation and non-profit management. In fact, **Playhouse Square Foundation is unique among American arts organizations for the extent of its involvement in urban redevelopment.**

In this vein, the Foundation makes history by leading the creation of the first Business Improvement District (BID) formally named "The Cleveland Theater District." (BID is a legal device which allows a defined area to self-assess and use the proceeds for the area's improvement.)

The Cleveland Theater District will undertake

security, maintenance and collective marketing, thereby supporting the goals of the District master plan. Several dozen Playhouse Square property owners and stakeholders join to promote passage of this legislation, which officially goes into effect in September of 1998.

1996

As the city of Cleveland begins the celebration of its 200th year, Bicentennial excitement is not lost on Playhouse Square Center, which boasts a bounty of personal reasons to celebrate.

Topping the list is the anticipation that 1996 will be the year Playhouse Square realizes another long-awaited goal: the entertaining of one million guests in a 12-month period at PSC! Those million-plus customers will be realized, thanks in part, to the National City Broadway Series' expansion to two weeks per production, initiated with the '96-'97 season. (**Cleveland will be one of only eight touring cities in the country boasting a two-week run for each Broadway booking on its series.**)

Above left: Artwork throughout the Wyndham Hotel highlights the rich theatrical heritage of Playhouse Square. Above right: A 50-ft. sculpture and multimedia light show, enhanced by special effects orchestrated to music, entertains visitors nightly in the Theater District.

STAR NOTES

During a 1936 engagement of **Ben Pollick** and his orchestra in the Ohio Theatre, a young trumpet player joined the band who was destined for future fame. His name was **Harry James**.

Above: Illuminated 'banners' are installed above the Ohio and State marquees in 1996.

1996 also begins the countdown of PSC theater birthdays... each one building to a final celebration in November of '97 when the Palace Theatre turns 75 years old. **February 5th** of '96 marks the 75th anniversary of the State Theatre, followed by the Ohio Theatre on **February 14th,** the nearby Hanna on **March 28th** and the Allen Theatre on April 1st. The Palace's original grand opening date of November 6th, will once again be cause to celebrate the milestone anniversary of the Center's completion back in 1922.

Much of the '96 excitement centers around the outside environs of Playhouse Square, beginning with an announcement that the Palace Theatre – the eastern gateway to Playhouse Square – will be crowned with a long-awaited marquee, via a generous gift from Playhouse Square Foundation Trustee Lois Horvitz.

The old marquee was razed and discarded 25-odd years ago anticipating the theater's demolition. As restoration began, the cost of building and installing a proper marquee was deemed financially prohibitive, with more urgent interior needs taking priority. Even though the Palace had been fitted with an electronic message-type marquee for its reopening in 1988, that marquee was never expected to be permanent.

So like a princess without a tiara, the exterior of the Palace gave no hint to the theater's interior splendor. All that changes the evening of October 23rd as guests and the media gather to watch Mrs. Horvitz throw the switch, premiering an eye-catching new Palace marquee. Graceful wings of bright metal and glass, plus colorful ribbons of neon punctuated by glowing bulbs, now create an exciting feeling of a royal arrival to Cleveland's "Palace".

Complementing the Palace's new marquee is the premiere of long-awaited 10-foot by 20-foot show banners to decorate the theater exteriors. The first three banners hung promote *Carousel,* The Ballet's *Nutcracker* and GLTF's *A Christmas Carol.* As these show banners herald upcoming Broadway and resident productions, they will serve a dual purpose: advertising as well as the addition of splashy color to the Theater District.

Above: The Palace Theatre
receives a new marquee,
in October of 1996, designed
by Thompson & Wood,
Cambridge, MA.

Above: A massive balloon launch heralds the dedication of Star Plaza, September 19, 1996. Below: Star Plaza becomes one of Cleveland's Bicentennial Legacy Projects.

Meanwhile, another "star" is welcomed to the District September 19th, at the dedication of Star Plaza. Mylar balloons in the shape of stars drop in a celestial shower from atop the Renaissance Building onto cheering crowds below.

The Governor, city officials and community leaders are present to offer congratulatory thanks to Star Bank, Playhouse Square Foundation, the State of Ohio, the Garden Club of Cleveland and the Shaker Lakes Garden Club, as well as the Cleveland Bicentennial Commission (which made Star Plaza one of its Bicentennial Legacy Projects during the 1996 celebrations).

The District is right on target with improvement plans. Next on the schedule will be dramatically lit billboards reminiscent of Broadway's Times Square, with plans to follow for a restaurant of note constructed within the Center. **But the grand finale, bar none, will be … the restoration of the Allen Theatre.**

The London Times visits Playhouse Square Center this year, as does the Mayor of Seattle and consultants representing clients in Australia. Their missions are: to study the remarkable phenomenon of Cleveland as an old industrial city which rallied around a vision of the future, giving new life to a theater district, which, in turn, became an integral part in reviving the city's dying downtown.

Meanwhile, in the limbic Allen Theatre, the venue's temporary cabaret space reopens September 26th for the premiere of the comic

murder mystery *Shear Madness.* Last season, when *Forever Plaid* initially reopened the Allen for business, audiences gained their first look at the deterioration effectuated during the many years since the Allen's closure.

Concurrently in the Center's other venues, contemporary programming offers a cavalcade of stars ranging from the magic of David Copperfield and pop music paragon Tony Bennett to Southern-styled rockers ZZ Top, (who trade their usual arena appearance in favor of treating fans to a rare small-hall concert … one that sells out in just one day!)

Cleveland's own hot New Age pianist/composer Jim Brickman, whose debut album has taken the music charts by storm, also performs his first Playhouse Square performance before a sold out hometown crowd.

And while the State Theatre again hosts B.B. King, "The King of the Blues", the Cleveland-San Jose Ballet's "blues" are turning to folding green as **the company's original composition entitled** *Blue Suede Shoes* **attracts national attention and critical acclaim.**

Left to right: Tony Bennett, Jim Brickman, and at right B.B. King. Inset: "Blue Suede Shoes" herald. Below: A digital remix of the original "Brel" cast is released on CD in 1996.

Blue Suede Shoes is performed to the music of Elvis Presley, sporting vibrant sets and glitzy costumes designed by Hollywood legend Bob Mackie. The red carpet rolls out for the production's premiere, attended not only by Mackie, but Presley's widow, Priscilla Presley, who lends her unqualified support to the production. **This creative, compelling work secures Cleveland Ballet's reputation as one of America's pre-eminent companies.**

A special reunion is about to take place in 1996: the original stars of PSC's *Jacques Brel Is Alive and Well and Living in Paris* return to the Center from various parts of the U.S. to celebrate the digital remix of their original cast album. Cliff Bemis, David O. Frazier, Providence Hollander and Theresa Piteo are joined by their original musical director David Gooding.

Clevelanders Joe Garry, Jr. ("Brel's" director and a reunion participant) and Carol Frankel, who co-produced the original "Brel" album, again join artistic forces on the remix, which is to be released for the first time on compact disc.

In August the Foundation kicks-off an ambitious Capital Campaign. Its goal is to raise $25 million: $15 million to renovate the Allen Theatre, and $10 million to establish a permanent endowment. The campaign promises to be one of the most far-reaching events of 1996, affecting the Center's operations past the coming millennium.

1997

A ground swell of excitement ushers in 1997, as the Center's wish list becomes reality in conjunction with exciting district changes and longtime goals met. **This is the celebratory year marking both the 75th anniversary of Playhouse Square Center, and the 25th Anniversary of the Playhouse Square Foundation.**

A fitting testimonial for this 75th celebration is not long in coming when, in January, the countdown begins to determine the Center's 10,000,000th guest! After each performance, attendance figures are diligently added to the aggregate attendance numbers.

Finally, on Tuesday, January 13th, an unsuspecting guest enters the Palace Theatre lobby for a production of *Damn Yankees.* She is greeted with fanfare declaring her "the 10,000,000th guest to attend Playhouse Square since its reopening". Television news cameras record her delighted reactions as she is presented with a multitude of gifts including a luxury cruise vacation. *Damn Yankees* star Jerry Lewis is present to offer his personal congratulations to the lucky lady.

Above: Jerry Lewis poses with the 10,000,000th guest to Playhouse Square Center. Below: Playhouse Square Center celebrates 75 years of entertainment.

A flurry of activity precedes the 75th celebration: committees are busy planning collateral anniversary events/tours and ordering commemorative 75th Anniversary items to be designed for sale at OHvations.

Raising glasses to toast PSC's 75th anniversary is complemented by a festive sparkling wine, bottled exclusively for the Playhouse Square celebration. An area-wide contest to select a winning label design for the PSC celebration champagne receives more than 200 artistic entries. The winning artist is Chris Cheetham. The Wyndham Hotel joins the salute by adopting the bubbly as its official house champagne for PSC's anniversary year.

Celebration events also move outside as the Playhouse Square Partners organization spearheads the

sale of personalized brick sidewalk pavers, the first of which are to be placed at the entrance of the Palace Theatre September 20th. This begins Phase One of a project that will eventually see messages "immortarized" on pavers installed in front of all four PSC theaters.

The Foundation ends fiscal '97 with announcement of a $1 million challenge grant by the Kresge Foundation of Troy, Michigan.

The grant requires the Foundation to raise $4.2 million by December 1998 to complete the challenge. PSF earmarks the monies toward construction of the Allen stagehouse and to secure a portion of the endowment for the capital campaign.

Meanwhile, exciting changes are in store for the Center's Ohio Theatre Lobby Cafe area. A national restaurateur has negotiated with the Foundation to remodel the Cafe space to house an upscale restaurant and provide catering facilities for planned reception rooms on the upper level.

The addition of a well-appointed area to host benefit dinners, parties, and wedding receptions has long been PSF's wish list. The dazzling twin marble staircases

Above left: Partners Leadership dedicates the first phase of the Partners' Promenade in front of the Palace Theatre, September 1997. Above right: The Ohio Theatre Outer Lobby Café in 1997, soon to be transformed into a new restaurant.

TRIVIA

In 1942 the Ohio Theatre became part of the war effort when the U.S. Coast Guard employed the venue's outer lobby as a recruiting office. Before the war in 1935, when the theater was turned into the Mayfair Casino, the Ohio sported the "World's Largest Bar", a grand, streamlined bar which seated 97 people. Its most expensive drink was a champagne cocktail for 75 cents. Martinis were 60 cents, and, if you wanted a meal with your cocktail, the most expensive item on the menu was filet mignon served with a mushroom sauce and fried potatoes for $2.25!

Above: The Hanna reopens in Fall of 1997 as a cabaret-style theater.

Opposite Page
Top: Longtitudinal section through Allen Theatre, (GSI Architects Inc.) Center and bottom: The old Allen Theatre stagehouse is demolished to make way for a new 'state of the arts' stage and supportive performance spaces, September 1997.

TRIVIA

The Hanna was built in 1921 by **Daniel Rhodes Hanna** in memory of his father, U.S. Senator **Marcus Alonzo Hanna**, who died in 1904. Mark Twain's *The Prince and The Pauper* starring William Faversham opened the venue March 28, 1921.

of the Palace Theatre consistently star as one of the most requested sites in Cleveland for bridal party photography. Now those brides are offered the opportunity to also utilize the Center for their reception festivities, thanks to the forthcoming catering and banquet facilities. The addition of this new restaurant and reception center is another step in the plan to add destination businesses to the heart of the Theater District.

As the Theater District opens its doors to a new establishment, it is poised to welcome back an old friend – the venerable Hanna Theatre. Amid champagne toasts from well wishers, the elegantly refurbished venue reopens its doors September 30th with a marquee lighting reception. Early Playhouse Square visionaries Lainie Hadden and Ray Shepardson are again the forces behind the Hanna's comeback as cabaret-seating venue which opens with *All Night Strut.*

But beyond the excitement of stellar entertainers and blockbuster shows ... beyond the festivities of the 75th Anniversary, an undercurrent of excitement pervades the celebration: realization that this will ultimately be the year for the long-awaited restoration of the Allen Theatre.

The story behind the Allen's rescue had suffered through the most protracted prologue of any of the Center's venues. The off-again, on-again status of the script receives a final re-write on **August 7th as Playhouse Square Foundation purchases the Allen and its surrounding land for $2 million.**

Unlike the Allen's previous crises, there is no need for an eleventh-hour reprieve on September 4th when a ceremonial swing of the wrecking ball signals not the final curtain for the once-elegant film palace,

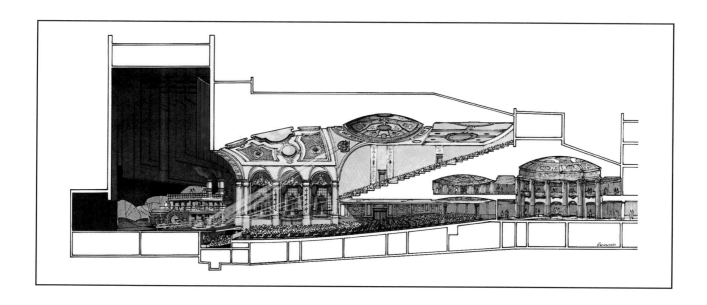

but rather "constructive" demolition for its rebirth.

PSF officials, long-standing friends of PSC and local media applaud a ceremony that sees perennial PSC supporters – the Cuyahoga County Commissioners – present a welcome $3 million check from the County to christen the Allen project.

Cleveland's Mayor Michael White joins in celebrating the Theater District's latest historic moment, and Congressman Louis Stokes is honored in absentia as one of the first Clevelanders to publicly promote and support the Allen project by helping to secure an early federal government grant.

The first step in the Allen restoration is demolition of the old "stagehouse" (a structure inadequate to house contemporary high-tech, large-scale productions for today's standards). Designed originally as a movie house, the venue was never meant to offer space for dressing rooms and scenery storage. The 77-year-old stagehouse bricks that crash to the ground from the wrecking ball's initial slam are only the first visible signs of the Allen production that has long been in "workshop".

In November, the Reinberger Foundation and the George and Pamela Humphrey Fund both step forward with significant pledges toward the Allen renovation. Major commemorations will be recognized in the finished Allen as a result of these pledges.

Above: Playhouse Square's resident companies are featured on a new illuminated billboard on the exterior wall of the Ohio Theatre as an outcome of the Cleveland Foundation's role in 1998. (Kapp & Associates, Inc.)

TRIVIA

In his biography *Mo Howard & The 3 Stooges* (Citadel Press), **Mo Howard** writes about the plight of dressing rooms on the road. Although dressing room accommodations were Spartan at best, hovels at worst, he notes that Playhouse Square's Palace Theatre (then in the RKO circuit) was an exception:

"This theater (the Palace) was built without missing thought for the actor's comfort. The Palace was beautiful not only outside and in the auditorium, but also backstage. Most impressive was the second floor of the theater, which sported a regulation-size pool table, chess tables, comfortable chairs, an ice machine and soft drinks, playing cards, cigars — it had all the facilities of a private club.

"In the basement was a laundry room complete with washing machines — no dryers in those day — while on the third floor were lines to spread and dry clothes, and warm air was piped in. There was even a nursery for youngsters. Best of all were the dressing rooms, heavily carpeted with mirrored walls and makeup tables. They had everything in them, right down to padded coat hangers."

1998

"Drama" is the byword for 1998. Theater-side drama for the fiscal year includes: an impressive 650 curtains, over 21,000 Broadway subscribers and – **for the second straight year – over one million guests entertained at the Center!**

Financial headlines are generated January 15th as Cleveland media assemble in the State Theatre lobby anticipating what PSF has cryptically hinted is "announcement of an historic partnership that will greatly impact the future of the theater district and its performing arts organizations".

Officials from PSF and the Cleveland Foundation jointly announce the **"largest single grant in the 84-year history of The Cleveland Foundation – $4 million to be awarded to Playhouse Square Foundation".** Terms of the grant will allow PSF to eliminate resident company rents over the next 10 years, and provide these companies with more identity within the Center.

The Cleveland Foundation's prominent role in the Center's history is recognized at this press conference, noting its financial aid in restoring the Ohio, State and Palace theaters and its involvement in helping the Cleveland Ballet, Cleveland Opera and Great Lakes Theater Festival to relocate to Playhouse Square Center.

In tandem with the press conference, media attendees are invited for a sneak peak into 1998's most visible drama unfolding at the Center. It is as compelling as any onstage production – the beginning of the Allen Theatre's renovation.

The Allen has endured countless incarnations. From its opening in 1921 as an ornate silent movie theater, it continued to entertain moviegoers, updated with new equipment as the technology demanded (i.e. in 1961 when stereo and a wide screen were added).

But as the populace moved to the suburbs, demands for downtown movie theaters waned, until the Allen screen went dark for the final time May 7, 1968. The venue was used for rock concerts from '73-'75, and then again as a "laserium" from 1977-'78.

During the "laserium" era, a restaurant also occupied the lobby and rotunda spaces, until 1982. In 1987, when building owners announced the Allen would be demolished the next year (to make way for a shopping/dining atrium and garage), it was the encore cry of "Save this theater!"… followed by déjà vu grumblings from the same contingent of nay-sayers who questioned whether a fourth restored theater was needed, let alone economically feasible.

Basking in the success of the renovated Ohio, State and Palace theaters, the Allen will answer its critics by finally providing the Center with a venue to host long-running musicals, thus allowing Cleveland to compete with New York and Toronto.

While the dream of a restored Allen Theatre begins to materialize, another of the Foundation's long-term goals materializes with the February opening of the elegant Ciao restaurant, located in the former Ohio Theatre Outer Lobby Café space.

PSF had worked tirelessly for years to attract a restaurateur of note to occupy this space. Months of redesign and renovation produce an elegant first-floor dining room and cafe-bar, plus a spacious second-floor, upscale banquet area (named "The Private Rooms of Playhouse Square") to accommodate up to 250 guests.

March 17th the former Founders' Club moves to spacious surroundings adjacent to the Private Rooms. It becomes the newest amenity for PSF and resident com-

Above: DANCECleveland presents Alvin Ailey American Dance Theater. Left: "Laserium" ticket. Below: Front entrance to Playhouse Square's newest restaurant, *Ciao!*, situated between the marquees of the Ohio and State Theatres.

Above left: The RJF
President's Club,
adjacent to the Private
Rooms of Ciao. Above
right: Roy H. Holdt
Boxholder's Lounge, in
the Palace Theatre. Left:
Commemorative Jacques
Brel plaque. Below:
Composer, Jacques Brel
(left) and Maddly Bamy.

pany Founder-level donors, renamed the "RJF President's Club", and made possible by the generosity of
long-time PSC supporter and trustee Richard J.
Fasenmyer. (The original Founders' Club space is updated and renamed the Roy H. Holdt Boxholders' Lounge,
to provide boxholders a special gathering area.)

March 13th becomes "lucky" Friday the 13th for
the Theater District: a ceremonial evergreen tree is hoist-
ed atop the newly completed Allen stagehouse skeleton,
signaling the official "topping off" of the structure.
Another milestone reached!

**Ironically, in 1971 the Allen had been the first of
the four orphaned PSC theaters to host the experiment
of bringing entertainment back to downtown. Now it is
the last of the quad to be saved and renovated.**

But the rescue and succeeding renovation of any of
the Center's venues might never have materialized without the success of *Jacques Brel Is Alive and Well and Living
in Paris*. To commemorate that show's 25th anniversary,
original cast members reunite at Playhouse Square on
the anniversary of *Brel's* April 18, 1973 premiere.

Joining the cast is founding Playhouse Square
Association President Lainie Hadden, and together

they dedicate a permanent Brel plaque in the State Theatre's lobby floor.

A special guest honors the anniversary reunion. Maddly Bamy, Jacques Brel's soul-mate for the last seven years of his life, arrives from Paris for the dedication (her first public appearance to celebrate the composer's work in the 20 years since his death).

Following the dedication, a sneak preview of the new workshop production of *Jacques and Maddly* is showcased. With music and lyrics by Bamy and Ann Mortifee, the production has been conceived and adapted by original *Brel* cast member David O. Frazier, plus original *Brel* director Joe Garry, Jr. and Mortifee.

In May, *Jacques and Maddly* performances in Kennedy's cabaret opens to the public. Guests are transported on a musical journey from France to the South Pacific, sharing the drama of composer *Brel's* final days in the company of Bamy and the specter of the late artist Paul Gauguin.

June 12th music extends beyond PSC'S walls to the adjacent Star Plaza as "Jazz Under the Stars" debuts. The after-work, happy-hour crowd will now be treated to plenty of jazz, food and festivities every

Above: The Jerry Bruno Band performs on Star Plaza during "Music Under the Stars," 1999-2000. Below: Horns and Things perform during the 1998 series "Jazz Under the Stars."

Top: Allen Theatre rotunda, 1998. Above: Maria Suter, of Evergreene Studios, New York City, masterfully applies details to the Allen Theatre's decorative ceilings.

Friday night throughout the summer.

It is now full steam ahead for ACT II of the Allen. Turner Construction and GSI Architects direct a talented cast of consultants and subcontractors. Their chorus of workers and artisans toil inside the auditorium restoring faded wall and ceiling artwork, creating molds to replace pieces from remaining original plasterwork and modernizing heating and electrical circuitry.

High drama continues during restoration. As flaking latex paint is removed from four auditorium ceiling areas, an exciting discovery comes to light ... **original Allen murals, injudiciously painted over, are revealed like lost Rembrandts hidden beneath cheap paintings.** Although this discovery translates into added work (the painstaking restoration of the original murals), the historic "find" cancels out any financial or time considerations.

Research into Allen architectural archives produces another surprise. Records describe the current 16 "painted" Corinthian columns of the Great Rotunda as "mahogany". When stripping restoration begins, workers discover the wood beneath is not mahogany but one of the most coveted woods in the world – black walnut! The happy discovery is likened to "mining for silver and discovering gold."

Media attention is legion for the Allen's restoration, but as reporters are paraded through the scaffolded, debris-strewn theater, all echo the same question: "Will this project actually be finished in time?"

By June, time-line fears are allayed with the announcement that the Allen is indeed "on time and on budget" for its October 2nd ribbon cutting. A Gala Committee, chaired by trustee K.K. Sullivan, is already hard at work planning an exclusive October 3rd opening benefit that promises to "rival any theater opening or party in the history of the Center".

October 2nd, amid a spectacular splash of fireworks and media attention, the Allen Theatre is poised to celebrate what might be called a "déjà vu debut." Mirroring its April 1, 1921 premiere, Clevelanders again crowd along Euclid Avenue,

Above: Restored ceiling and murals in Allen Theatre auditorium, 1998. Below: Ceiling of Allen Theatre auditorium, 1997, prior to discovery of hidden paintings.

Above: Playhouse Square officials and civic dignitaries pull together to unveil the Allen Theatre's renovated canopy. Below: Crowds gather in front of the Allen Theatre for a ribbon cutting and unveiling ceremony, October 2, 1998.

cavorting in a festive street party that precedes their first peek into the elegantly refurbished venue.

Excitement mounts and TV cameras roll as Ohio Governor George Voinovich, his wife Janet, an impressive list of dignitaries and proud Playhouse Square Foundation officials and supporters cut the Allen's ceremonial red ribbon.

One dream ... 25 years ... sundry setbacks ... innumerable volunteer and worker hours ... and ... $53 million dollars later, the collective prayers of Playhouse Square's early visionaries are answered: the final piece of the Center's reconstruction puzzle is set in place.

A surprise pyrotechnic explosion heralds the magical disappearing act of a mammoth crimson tarp veiling the Allen's façade. Voila! The elegant "new" Allen canopy (true to its original 1921 design) is revealed. Lobby doors swing open to welcome an awestruck standing-room-only crowd. They file in to inspect the lavish mirrored lobby, the intricate architecture of the Great Rotunda and the plush auditorium with its art-laden ceilings.

Left (and cover page): The new Allen Theatre Marquee is revealed, surrounded by a sensational ring of pyrotechnics. Below: Wyndham Hotel is silouhetted by a musically orchestrated fireworks display. Bottom: Gala guests revel as they witness the historic celebratory program in the restored Allen Theatre auditorium, October 3, 1998.

Above: Dancers from Cleveland Museum of Art perform under the Allen Theatre's restored canopy. Inset: Commemorative "Light the Lights" playbill. Below: Playhouse Square President, Art Falco, initiates a 'champagne waterfall.'

Following their sneak peek, these Allen first-nighters return to the street celebration for yet another visual treat: a grand finale of eye-popping fireworks-set-to-Broadway-show tunes which explode in cascades from atop the Wyndham Hotel.

But this pyrotechnic finale is hardly a denouement to the Allen's celebration. The theater's unofficial kick-off had actually taken place the evening before when the cast of architects and tradesmen who had toiled on the renovation were invited to join PSC employees for their own champagne preview inside the Allen.

A special musical slide presentation celebrates a job well done via time-lapse visuals of the venue's progress – from the first wrecking ball blow to the old stagehouse to the final brush stroke and carpet tack. More than a few tradesmen admit to a lump in the throat and a prideful tear in the eye as they watch their contributions unfold on the screen.

One master plaster worker confides that, for him, the Allen project has been a labor of love, "Something artistic and tangible that my grandkids can show their grandkids, and know that **I** was proud to be a part of this beautiful restoration."

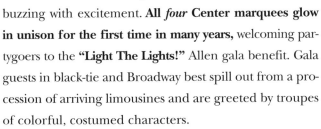

The evening of October 3rd finds Euclid Avenue again buzzing with excitement. **All *four* Center marquees glow in unison for the first time in many years,** welcoming par-tygoers to the **"Light The Lights!"** Allen gala benefit. Gala guests in black-tie and Broadway best spill out from a pro-cession of arriving limousines and are greeted by troupes of colorful, costumed characters.

Once inside, the focal point of the evening turns to the Allen's Great Rotunda, where the world-famous Moët and Chandon Champagne Pyramid has been assembled. The crystal champagne glasses which com-prise the 12-foot high tower have been flown in from

France specifically for the opening. **(This celebratory pyramid has been assembled only one time prior in the United States!)**

As the final trickle of bubbly flows from the pyramid's summit to its base, gala-goers withdraw to the Allen auditorium to savor the honor of being the first audience to experience an official performance in the elegantly restored venue.

Broadway's quintessential Tommy Tune royally christens the Allen's expansive stage as the benefit's featured entertainer. "Grand" finale becomes an understatement when an historic collaboration of talent from the Center's resident companies (Cleveland Opera, Cleveland-San Jose Ballet, DANCECleveland, Dancing Wheels, Great Lakes Theater Festival, Ohio Ballet) join the 170-member Ohio University Marching Band in a memorable salute, complete with unexpected explosions of onstage fireworks.

At the final applause, OU Marching Band members lead the audience in a Pied Piper egress up the

Above: Gala guests gather to witness the world-famous Moët and Chandon Champagne Pyramid in the Allen Theatre rotunda.
Left: Tommy Tune.
Below: Performers gather on the Allen Theatre stage for the Gala's Grand Finale.

Top: Rod puppets created by Rocky River High School students, in partnership with the Cleveland Museum of Art's *"Parade the Circle,"* participate in Palooza. Above: The Cleveland Institute of Music hosts an 'instrument petting zoo'. Below: Master chalk muralist, Kurt Wenner.

aisles, out onto the street and into the Ohio, State and Palace theaters for the next festive leg of the celebration.

The stages and lobbies of the Center's venues are elegantly decorated and bathed in a shimmer of twinkle lights, transforming the areas into baronial dining halls for a memorable sit-down gourmet dinner. The celebration continues into the early hours as guests dance throughout the complex to ongoing music from jazz, rock and Motown bands.

One of those bands, the venerable Tex Beneke Orchestra, entertains, adding to its own Playhouse Square history: Tex Beneke and his Orchestra had not only played at the gala reopening of the Palace Theatre in 1988, Beneke had performed there two generations earlier as part of the famous Glenn Miller Orchestra.

The excitement of "Light The Lights!" is exceeded only by its purpose: to donate gala proceeds to the Foundation's endowment to benefit educational programs for people of all ages. To this end, the gala raises an amazing **$1,000,405 … the most successful Cleveland benefit to date!**

The morning after, staff and volunteers – still running on adrenaline – trade tuxes and gowns for T-shirts and tennis shoes to host one of the largest arts celebrations the city has ever seen – an event dubbed **Palooza!** (It is hosted by the Center's new Education Department, which had been formed in August.)

Palooza! offers up a free-of-charge day for the general public to: tour the new Allen and its three sister theaters (including rare backstage visits); attend performances by local artists and resident companies; take part in hands-on entertainment experiences such as the musical instrument "petting zoo"; enjoy a variety of youngsters' craft making stations and educational opportunities; and marvel at a three-dimensional sidewalk painting created over a four-day span by master street painter Kurt Wenner.

The day is designed to bring home the message **that Playhouse Square belongs to the entire community** … and that community comes out in force, over 8000 strong! (With its positive feedback, **Palooza!** is such a resounding success that it becomes an easy decision to make it an annual event.)

Palooza! is a fitting finale to the four-day marathon of activities surrounding the Allen. But the eminence of the Allen's reopening carries more significance than just the celebration of its rescue and successful restoration.

With the Allen's 2,504 seats added to the Center's existing 7,155 seats, Playhouse Square Center's capacity of 9,659 now qualifies it as the **"second-largest performing arts center in North America"** right behind New York City's Lincoln Center. Completion of the Allen is also the final puzzle piece in what has been **the world's largest theater restoration project!**

October 1998 will be remembered as a pivotal month in PSC annals. Not only does the restoration finale of the four venues meld the Center's "past" to its "present", but a giant step into the "future" is on the horizon: Playhouse Square Center takes the on-ramp to the Information Highway in October, **debuting its exciting new website: www.playhousesquare.com.**

It is to be one of the most significant changes in live entertainment since computerized ticketing. The website's state-of-the-art information and ticketing services will revolutionize the way the Center can reach out to its guests, while proposed interactive features will allow guests to respond in kind.

(In its first year, the PSC website wins a national award and gains the applause of both information-seeking guests and online ticket-purchasing guests. It effectively relegates those snaking box office lines of the past to dinosaur status. Each day the website continues to make the "future" the "present".)

The website's first show available for online ticketing is *Jolson* (the story of singer Al Jolson). *Jolson* wins the

www.playhousesquare.com

Above: Playhouse Square Centers new website: www.playhousesquare.com Below: "Jolson" playbill.

Above: Allen Theatre auditorium, 1998. Below: Cleveland Orchestra 1998-1999 program.

hat trick when it comes to "firsts". In addition to being the first show online, the musical taps the Center to be the first stop as it kicks off its national road tour. **Jolson also becomes the first official booking to play the newly-opened Allen.** (Ironically, *Jolson* opens on the anniversary of the premiere of the first "talkie" film feature, *The Jazz Singer*, which starred Al Jolson.)

Singer Mary Chapin Carpenter takes home the honor of "first concert performance" in the Allen. Hot on her heels is Broadway's *Footloose*, a stage treatment of the hot 1984 movie, and **the second musical this season to choose Playhouse Square's Allen Theatre to debut its national tour.**

A duo of financial high notes completes 1998. November 3rd brings announcement of a $300,000 challenge grant, awarded to PSF by the GAR Foundation of Akron. The grant will require the Foundation to raise $600,000 in new pledges toward its capital campaign by December 1999.

Meanwhile, the $1 million Kresge Foundation challenge grant awarded PSF in December 1997 had set a goal of $4.2 million, to be raised by the end of calendar '98. Playhouse Square meets that eligibility late in December.

Year's end finds the Foundation poised to duplicate its internal financial successes by turning its focus on the Cleveland Theater District. An important acquisition comes as a result of a donation of the One Playhouse Square Building by Mid-America Management, headed by Alan M. Krause. The Foundation will now evaluate alternatives for redevelopment of the 220,000 square-foot building located on the west side of the Allen.

Above: One Playhouse Square Building, 1375 Euclid Avenue. Below: Hanna Theatre upper level side box.

1999

March 1st becomes noteworthy as PSC enthusiastically welcomes the world-renowned Cleveland Orchestra. While its Severance Hall residence undergoes renovation, the Orchestra will call the new Allen "home" through the end of '99. Another orchestra, the Cleveland Pops Orchestra, also entertains with four concerts in the Ohio Theatre.

While PSF celebrates with **a balanced budget for the 11th consecutive fiscal year,** the Foundation is in negotiations for what could prove to be a pivotal real estate acquisition for the Theater District...the purchase of the Hanna Building.

On August 24th, papers to seal the purchase are

Above: Facades of the Wyndham Hotel (left) and the Hanna Building (right) are selected as sites to install fiber optics, LED video boards and a 'news ticker.' (Animation Graphics, NY) Below: The Hanna Theatre marquee.

finally signed by an investor group headed by the Foundation. Not only does this acquisition aid the Foundation in its continuing challenge to mold the District, **the purchase carries a significant theatrical plus – ownership of the historic Hanna Theatre.** (The Hanna had again closed following a brief 11-month revival).

With the Allen's renovation, it was assumed the final puzzle piece was now in place, completing the jig-saw picture of four historic theaters. Suddenly a fifth theater is welcomed into the PSF family of venues, and research begins to find the best entertainment use for this newest acquisition.

Control of the Hanna Building now benefits another PSF long-range goal for the Theater District: the mounting of giant video boards on district build-ings, creating an atmosphere of Times Square. (The video boards are scheduled to premier next year, adding color and news tickers to the area surround-ing Star Plaza.)

NEW MILLENNIUM ARRIVES

2000

Below: Downtown Cleveland Partnership develops a plan to revitalize Euclid Avenue, which includes upscale condominiums and a vibrant mix of retail in the Playhouse Square area.

T HE YEAR BEGINS WITH A DECIDED WINNER...a four-time Tony Award winner...as the Allen stage becomes the great ship *Titanic* for a musical drama collage of stories about its ill-fated passengers. Dance aficionados flock to see Broadway's *Fosse* as well as a quick-selling return of *Stomp*. *Miss Saigon* heads to the Allen for an extended run, while historical periods are set to music with the productions of *Ragtime* and *The Civil War*.

On the concert scene, hot new Latino heartthrob Marc Anthony draws a vocal standing-room-only crowd to the Allen. He is followed two days later

Left to right: Engelbert Humperdinck, Marc Anthony, Michael Bolton and Al Green. Below: "Tony 'n' Tina's Wedding" opens at the Hanna Theatre, September 2000 (Ray Ficca and Lisa Ray).

in the Allen by veteran pop singer Engelbert Humperdinck who, at 62, is still a heartthrob to the many fans who ring the stage during his concert.

Andrew Lloyd Webber dominates the Summer of 2000 as the extended run of the phenom *Phantom* hangs its chandelier in the Allen for the first time. Only days after *Phantom* departs, another ALW booking opens at the Palace with Michael Bolton included in the cast of *The Music of Andrew Lloyd Webber.*

Music of yet another showbusiness legend comes to life July 18th for a week of *Buddy: The Buddy Holly Story*, and other summer music at PSC entertains via Boney James' jazz, and veteran and newcomer R&B acts: Al Green and Mary J. Blige.

The surprise attendance hit of the summer is PSC's third "Cinema at the Square", a month-long celebration of classic American films. Cartoons, "shorts", the sounds of the mighty Kimball organ and the largest non-IMAX screen in Ohio combine to recreate the by-gone atmosphere of movie-going with films ranging from *Casablanca* to *West Side Story.*

With the 2000-2001 season on the horizon, the Center looks to increase the number of performances for its now "five" venues, including a booking of the interactive comedy *Tony 'n' Tina's Wedding* as the first PSC-sponsored show to play the newly-acquired Hanna Theatre.

September 7th the Hanna's marquee comes alive once more as *Tony 'n' Tina's Wedding* premieres to a capacity number of "nuptial guests". Cleveland would now discover why this wedding/reception spoof has enjoyed five to 10-year runs in cities like New York, Chicago and Minneapolis.

Within two weeks of its opening, *Tony 'n' Tina's Wedding* sells out its initial four-month booking, with – at this printing – no end in sight to the now open-ended run.

Added opportunity for combining entertainment with education to benefit every facet of the community becomes the new decade's priority for PSF. As the second-largest performing arts center in the nation, PSC remains a driving force, continuing to shape both the Theater District and Cleveland's entertainment scene.

That entertainment tableau has followed an amazing evolution, born from its first humble Public Square tavern performance in 1820 Cleveland, where actors performed, illuminated only by candles and gaslights.

How could those entertainers and their audiences ever envision today's performing arts climate? Rife with the high-tech venues which currently comprise the thriving downtown Theater District, each season premieres more eye-popping special effects and added sophistication in audio.

What Cleveland Opera House performer circa 1875 could imagine an opera audience aided in their understanding of the performance by the projection of translated lyrics?

How could dance companies envision the day when its dancing surface would be composed of shock-absorbing layers that are bone-and-muscle friendly?

What theatergoer in the year 1900 dared believe a time would come when hearing-challenged patrons would be able to hear and enjoy a performance thanks to technological aids?

Today's symbiotic relationship between the past and the future bears witness to an anachronistic scene: patrons seated in a 1920s theater admiring art work inspired by another century, yet holding a ticket that

Above: Cleveland School of the Arts, "Youth At Risk Dancing" (YARD) conduct a community workshop and perform on the Allen Theatre stage during Palooza 2000. Below: The Playhouse Square Center website invites visitors to take a virtual walking tour of the theaters, www.playhousesquare.com.

was selected and purchased on a 21st century computer screen linked by space-age technology to a website.

Although the new millennium finds us reviewing the evolution of Cleveland's entertainment venues, we mourn those great theaters that have been lost to either fire or the wrecking ball. We are, however, fortunate that five of the Theater District's historic venues have prevailed.

On that note, it is fitting that the latest update of this Cleveland entertainment chronicle (referred to in its original printing as *The Redbook*) take its leave.

An appropriate epilogue is borrowed from excerpts of a letter that Foundation President Art J. Falco was asked to compose for the City of Cleveland's Bicentennial. The letter, along with a variety of entertainment memorabilia representative of the PSC theaters, was placed in the Bicentennial Time Capsule in 1996. When the seal is broken and the capsule opened in the year 2096, Cleveland will begin the celebration of its Tercentennial, and – hopefully – Playhouse Square will be preparing to celebrate the 175th Anniversary of its completion.

President Falco's time capsule letter contemplates the 2096 arts & entertainment scene with thought-provoking questions – answers to which will be revealed only to our descendants:

• What will be the state of entertainment and the arts 100 years into the future? Will it be funded privately or publicly?

• Will "live" performances, as we know them today, endure, or will the "virtual reality" form of entertainment currently in its infancy replace them?

• Will entertainment and the arts play a greater or lesser role in the lives of Clevelanders in the year 2096?

Whatever the outcome, Clevelanders can take pride in the stellar success of having preserved an integral part of the city's entertainment history and architecture. The rescue and restoration of the Allen, Ohio, State, Palace and Hanna theaters has provided a tangible link to our past and a quintet of marquees to light our performing arts future.

Not "The End"…merely "An Intermission."

Above: Craig Woodson rallies Palooza 2000 participants to the Allen Theatre stage for the "Pop Goes Palooza!" grand finale. Below: Dancers from original Broadway cast of "Swing!" perform during Palooza 2000.

PHOTO CREDITS & ACKNOWLEDGEMENTS

WRITTEN AND EDITED BY:

Kathleen Kennedy (1810-1975 copy);

Jean Emser Schultz (1975-2000 copy)

Art direction/computer graphics: Type & Design, Luanne Stewart

Photo research/editing: Ruth Flannery

Printing: Activities Press Inc.; Binding: Riverside Group

HISTORICAL PHOTOGRAPHS COURTESY OF:

The Cleveland Orchestra Archives (The Heiser Co.); The Cleveland Photograph Collection of the Cleveland Public Library (Crowley-Stokes); The Cleveland Press Collection; Euclid Avenue Association (courtesy of Donald Grogan); Ohio Historical Society; Photographs of Yesteryear (Bruce Young); Rapp & Rapp Collection (Chicago Historical Society); David Thum Collection; Theatre Historical Society of Elmhurst, Illinois; and the Western Reserve Historical Society, Cleveland, Ohio.

HISTORICAL MATERIALS COURTESY OF:

Mrs. Evelyn K. Blum; The Cleveland Public Library, Literature Department; Weldon Carpenter; Charles van Dijk; Elizabeth Fitz Gerald; Frank J. Frischauf Family; Mrs. Robert I. Gale, Jr.; Virginia Heidloff; Ron Hendzel; Frank Kirbus; Rebecca Kurber; Linda Kirk; *Marquee Magazine* (courtesy of B. Andres Corsini); Mrs. Fred R. White; Mrs. Nancy Young; The William Myers Collection; Joseph Pales; *The Plain Dealer*, Cleveland, Ohio; the Playhouse Square Archives Collection and the Western Reserve Historical Society.

PHOTOGRAPHY CREDITS:

Alfred Associates; David Behl; Robert Bellamy; Marc Braun (Braun Photography); Cleveland Opera (Dirk Bakker); Cleveland San Jose Ballet; The Cleveland Theater District; Don Curran and Wm. Gesten (Foto Arts, Inc.); DANCECleveland; Michael Edwards; M. Fawick; Great Lakes Theater Festival; Michael Hauser; Kehres Photo; Bruce Keifer; Janet Macoska; Roger Mastroianni; Bill Nehez; Larry Nighswander; Tom Prusha; The Richards Group, Wyndham Playhouse Square Hotel; Bruce Schwartz; Ray Shepardson; and David Thum.

BIBLIOGRAPHY:

Bell, Archie, *A Journey Through B. F. Keith's Palace Theatre*, 1922.

Callister Robert, *The Official Playhouse Square Center Tourguide's Guidebook*, 1999.

Rose, William Ganson, *Cleveland: The Making of a City*, World Publishing Co., Cleveland & New York, 1950.

Time-Life, Inc., *This Fabulous Century*, Prelude and Vols. 1-7, 1969-1975.

Wilson, Ella Grant, *Famous Old Euclid Avenue of Cleveland*, 1932.

SPECIAL THANKS TO:

Luanne Stewart (Type & Design); Rachel Abbey, Art Falco, Jennifer Gaglione, John Hemsath and Jim Szakacs (Playhouse Square Foundation); Mary Strassmeyer & Jake Rosenheim (*The Plain Dealer*); Dick Wooten and Bob Love (*The Cleveland Press*); Janet Coe Sanborn, Herbert Mansfield and Evelyn Ward (Cleveland Public Library); M. M. Bubbles, Dottie McNulty; Barbara deConingh; Richard Sklenar (Theater Historical Society of Elmhurst, Illinois); John Grabowski, Virginia Hawley and Richard Manual (Western Reserve Historical Society).

VERY SPECIAL THANKS TO:

Neil J. Van Uum and Joseph-Beth Group for their help and enthusiasm in marketing and publishing this book.

CHAIRMEN OF PLAYHOUSE SQUARE FOUNDATION
(in order of service):

Oliver C. Henkel, Jr.

John F. Lewis

Julien L. McCall

Forrest D. Hayes

Glenn R. Brown

Jon H. Outcalt

Henry F. Eaton